Back to Basics

Donald Quinn

Edited By Polia Quinn and Bethany Wood

AuthorHouse™
1663 Liberty Drive
Bloomington, IN 47403
www.authorhouse.com
Phone: 1-800-839-8640

© 2012 by Donald Quinn. All rights reserved.

No part of this book may be reproduced, stored in a retrieval system, or transmitted by any means without the written permission of the author.

Published by AuthorHouse   03/27/2012

ISBN: 978-1-4685-7439-5 (sc)
ISBN: 978-1-4685-7442-5 (e)

Library of Congress Control Number: 2012905698

Any people depicted in stock imagery provided by Thinkstock are models, and such images are being used for illustrative purposes only.
Certain stock imagery © Thinkstock.

This book is printed on acid-free paper.

Because of the dynamic nature of the Internet, any web addresses or links contained in this book may have changed since publication and may no longer be valid. The views expressed in this work are solely those of the author and do not necessarily reflect the views of the publisher, and the publisher hereby disclaims any responsibility for them.

Table of Contents

The Journey's Beginning 1
Passion 3
Passion 6
Competency 7
Competency 10
The Sweet Spot 12
Back To Basics: A Journey Not A Destination 17
Culture 18
Attitude 22
Leading Cultural Change 24
Values 27
Change 28
Change 30
Influencing Change 37
Listen Learn Change 40
The Team 43
The Lessons 44
Character Of The Team 46
Clear Goal Setting 47
Communicate Till It Hurts 48
Self-Accountability 49
Leadership Styles 50
Effects Of The Team 53
Advancing Competence 55
The Peter Principle 55

Career Trees And Paths 57
Organizational Structure 59
Core Competency 62
Competencies For Advancement 65
Behavioral Identifiers 66
Talking An Employee Into A Position 68
Talking An Employee Through A Position 68
Talking An Employee Out Of A Position 70
Leadership 72
Influence 74
Intellect 75
Commitment 76
Vision 77
Image 78
Thinking On Your Feet 80
Leadership Styles 82
Time And Time Management 85
Customer Service 96
Motivation 108
Types And Time Of Motivation 114
Landscapes Of Failure 120
The Forest 122
The Desert Mirage 124
The Quagmire 125
The Mountain 127
The Raging River 128
Bunny Trails 130
Land Of The Magic Bullet 131
A Final Word 133
Bibliography 137

The Journey's Beginning

> *"The woods are lovely, dark, and deep,*
> *But I have promises to keep,*
> *And miles to go before I sleep,*
> *And miles to go before I sleep."*
> —Robert Frost

It should be noted that when I have the time I am completely addicted to Facebook, to the point where I actually have the application installed on my I Phone. The reason I bring this up is recently one of those mindless surveys was making the rounds again. You know the kind, that asks you a million and one, semi-private questions and then to complete the circle of pain insists that you post it and tag all your friends so that they now have the torturous task of reading all about you and/or completing it themselves. This is something we all love to hate but when bored enough will fill out anyway. And so being that bored late one night while taking a break from writing, I decided to fill the thing out. A handful of questions into it, the article finally posed one question that caused me pause and actually think. The question was "What did you want to be when you grow up?"

As simple and almost mindless as that seems it raised, in my mind, a real dilemma because over the course of the years I had lost touch with the child who had wild and romantic dreams of the things he wanted to become. As a matter of fact, the two of us probably wouldn't even get along very well as I can see myself scolding him to be a realist. But here we are so many years later, staring at a computer screen trying to remember which one of the million fantasy careers was the one that most stuck out in my mind. The question I kept asking myself was why is it so important for me to remember what I wanted to be, and then it struck me. While we all have childish ideas of growing up and become a superhero or perhaps saving the world with our epic inventions, very few of us actually see those dreams turn into any sort of reality. Instead we allow our lives to take hold of our destinies and race us on a helter skelter course towards retirement and old age. Each day that passes concerned about mortgages, car payments and whether Susie in the next cubical is going to get that promotion instead of me, takes us a little further away from pirates and buried treasure. Amazingly we also find ourselves not quite as happy as we were when we were children filled with dreams and the hopes of tomorrow, instead consoling ourselves with shallow victories taken in our adult lives. Where once we dreamed of doing amazing things, now we will pat ourselves on the back for getting a small raise or extra vacation week from a job we hate.

As a boy I was quite torn with what I wanted to accomplish in my lifetime. First I wanted to be a medical missionary who would go into the deepest regions of the Amazon to bring health and teaching to the native tribes that lived there. Then I wanted to be a multibillionaire tycoon who owned a huge corporation of ships and was quite debonair. Finally, like many boys I wanted to be a spy with super powers who saves the world from unforeseen dastardly things. In my mind they all made perfect sense and eventually I was able to club them all together into a multibillionaire superspy who used his medical training as a cover while teaching tribal people. Unrealistic! Of course that was the whole point. But let us pause for a second and find out what these childish ideas really say about who I am at the very core of my being before pouring on the layers of maturity and adult reasoning.

First the idea of using medicine indicated an early love of healing and helping people, the idea of going to medical school to achieve it, however, quickly put a damper on that one. What is important to note is that I have always wanted to help people. Second, teaching people came naturally. Being the child of a teacher it was in the blood and the idea of imparting knowledge is still something I truly enjoy doing. Third, I wanted to make a lot of money and realized even then that there had to be a method to earning that money. Trade, or in other words a world of business was the oyster in which I would find my pearl. And while I have not gone on to be a billionaire there is still a deep love for the way business works. Put the four things together and you get

- Healing / Helping People
- Teaching and Imparting Knowledge
- Business Leadership
- Make Money

I skipped over the super spy bit because that was true childish fantasy and it is important to leave childish things behind when thinking like an adult. This has to be duly noted so that no one gives up their high paying 9 to 5, dons a cape and then blames me for their lack of flight (or food).

Ask yourself, "What did you want to be when you grew up?" Allow yourself to spend a moment in that imaginative place where finances and responsibilities don't exist. The only thing there are, are dreams.

Passion

"There is no passion to be found playing small—in settling for a life that is less than the one you are capable of living."—Nelson Mandela

This is an exercise I encourage everyone reading this to perform. Who we are as people tends to define what we will be successful at. For example very few small business owners go into business because they feel that the business will make them overnight success stories, rather most go into business because they find a product or service that they absolutely fall in love with. That childish passion which remains dormant within us through all the years of adulthood eventually does find an outlet. It is up to us to ensure that we are doing things that we are fundamentally passionate about.

Every journey starts somewhere and has a definite direction. The journey to success is no different and it is highly likely that many of us have several false starts along the way. What is important to note about this book is that this is not a book that gives you the answers to the questions or provides you with some deep knowledge that you otherwise would have remained oblivious to. Much to the contrary this is about taking the very basics, things we already know, and remembering that every great story begins with once upon a time. Things you will read are simply a foundation for building a stronger organization, recreating structure from chaos and most importantly getting down to brass tacks. The place where the rubber meets the road is where it all happens, always has and always will. Just like life journeys through adulthood take us far from the child we all hold in such fond memory, so too does time age our professional and corporate dreams. Whether this book is the start of a personal journey or a professional realignment every step begins with passion.

Having asked yourself what you wanted to be when you grew up and taking a few moments to reminiscence or wander down memory lane, we come to the next phase of identifying passion. Passion is a strange emotion that springs from multiple sources, making it paramount to understand what core passions we can then turn into actionable and non-cape wearing realities. In order to dig deeper the question "why?" takes on a key role.

For example, if you wanted with all your heart to be a doctor when you grew up, you pestered your parents for the doctor set and made all your friends submit to being jabbed with a blunt syringe. The question you have to ask as an adult recapturing passion is why. What was it about being a doctor that drove you to wanting to be the man or woman with the medicine? There are several answers, the easiest one could be you simply loved medicine and were fascinated by illness. In which case stop reading and find out how to get into school to study infectious disease. Another positive answer could be because you wanted to help people, which is a passion. Negative reasoning could be you wanted to be a doctor because you liked how stately and professional the coats and stethoscope looked—making the passion image and prestige. While there is nothing wrong with either of those neither of them can truly be translated into the business world of actionable items.

The important thing to do is to write down what you are passionate about, starting with your earliest childhood dreams and working your way up to today. No idea is too silly to skip. That is what the filtering process is for. I believe that many people, I would venture most people, will find that the things they were passionate about as children are still the core passions which fulfill them today. Once you have narrowed it down to three or four key items, keep them handy as they will be used in the next few exercises. Having more than three or four is not bad for hobbies, when dealing with actionable passions it is rare for someone to have many; so if you find yourself with a dozen after filtering with why, pick the top four or five.

Passion! Write it on a blank piece of paper and draw a large circle under it. Then write the items you identified as your passions in the circle, so that it looks something like this

PASSION

- Healing / Helping People
- Teaching
- Business Leadership
- Making Money

Now you know what things make you happy, what you are truly passionate about doing. Here's a little life secret, unless you are the most optimistic person on earth you will never be happy unless you are fulfilling at least one of these passions in your professional life. We spend most of our waking hours at work and as such need to be in a place where our passion meets our profession in order to have an ounce of true satisfaction.

Ironically companies are born from their passion, things which the founders got fired up about. As a company, however, it is easy to let the minutia take control and lose sight of the primary vision which started the journey. Hence it is equally important for company managers to perform a "passion" evaluation periodically through the companies' life cycle. The question one needs to ask is "what are we passionate about?" and later on "Are we still passionate about the same things?"

I launched a marketing company in India in 1997. We did campaigns for corporations like HP, Compaq, Channel V (VHI India) and others. We experienced rapid growth in clients and employees and after the first year had to stop, breath and evaluate where we were at and how to move forward. We took a couple days and as a management team reviewed our past and pondered our future. As we were reevaluating our course, we came up with three things that we were extremely passionate about. These were the ideas that had brought us together and had literally defined who we were up until the point where we were debating our future path. These three things were

- Project Management
- Data
- Saving Clients Money

When was the last time you and your team reviewed what you are passionate about? It is important to do because a team unified and going in the same direction will accomplish amazing things. A disjointed team will be sluggish and slow maybe eventually arriving at the desired destination. For example if you as a manager are passionate about something for the business that your team cares nothing about you will have a big problem. Your passion and vision will not be implemented, there will be misunderstandings and everyone will be frustrated.

Competency

"Ability will never catch up with the demand for it"—Confucius

While we are on the subject of secrets here is another one. What we are passionate about doing may differ greatly from what we are good at doing. Skill sets and raw ability are key elements to our success in the working world. We learn this too from a very early age when the smarter kids and the ones who study harder do better in school. Natural God given talent aside, there are those of us who work very hard at getting good at something. There is little need to point out that if you are truly passionate about something, learning how to do it well becomes a whole lot easier. Quite frankly without passion we would rarely engage in extra learning and when we do it is typically and un-enjoyable process.

What am I good at doing? That is the second question of the day. Again it is important not to set limits or to allow yourself to be cornered by what it is you find yourself doing currently. What you are good at, your core competencies, are things that manifest on a consistent basis. Reflect on your professional and personal life. What traits stand out regardless of what you are doing? What do you gravitate toward and choose to spend your time on? Your core strengths are things that you will do regardless of whether they are in your job description. For example if design is a core competency you may find yourself spending time creating a marketing flyer to show customers even though your actual job description is to do sales. Instead of asking your marketing director to design it, you do it yourself. Your top competencies are things that come naturally to you and when being used things feel easier.

These brain storming sessions have everything to do with you as an individual or you as a corporate entity. As a company owner or a manager you should be asking a second question. The question should be, "What are _we_ good at doing?" ensuring that your talents are not the only ones being pondered. Honestly evaluating and understanding your teams competencies will assist you as an owner and manager to determine where your team should spend their time and who on the team should complete specific tasks. Operating with this perspective will help you accomplish task faster and meet your goals. It will also ensure that your employees will be have greater job satisfaction and be less frustrated in their daily work.

When I spent time evaluating my core competencies I found key things kept popping up. For me the answers were many fold, there are a lot of things I consider myself good at, though, my wife would probably smirk at a few of them like mowing the grass (we'll just cross that one off the list for now). Instead let's focus on real life actionable things which may be done every day and ultimately might just keep my otherwise idle hands, or idle employees, from doing non-productive things. After a process of writing down all the ideas that came to mind down I came up with five things that I find myself "good at" in a professional sense.

- Writing
- Listening
- Teaching
- Team Building
- Leadership

Just so that this is not only an exercise in personal journey, I did this part of the exercise with my marketing company as wel. All the management participated and after much debate we came up with three key things we were good at doing

- Sales
- Project Management
- Advertising campaigns

This was a revelation for us because until this time we had been a data base and direct mail advertising business. When we conducted this exercise we had very grudgingly completed an advertising campaign project for a long standing customer and were debating if this was where we needed to go. Needless to say the answers were unexpected and changed who we were as a company.

Let us go back to the personal exercise. While a million things make me who I am, things that are fundamental to my every day, there are some things which are core to who I am. These things I do naturally and in turn they force other events to take place. For example, in a room full of people I will naturally assume a leadership role which in turn leads to team building. Other skills which competed for the top spots were things like time management, but this is a skill I have had to learn over a decade of meeting deadlines and so could not be considered part of my core skill sets. Honesty, regardless of whether this is a personal or a corporate exercise, is vital to truly digging deep and knowing what you are good at doing.

Once you have narrowed it down to core competencies it is time to take another piece of paper and draw a large circle with the header competency, just like this.

COMPETENCY

- Writing
- Listening

- Teaching
- Team Building
- Leadership
- Healing / Helping People
- Teaching
- Business Leadership
- Making Money

In the span of a few hours two things become very clear. The first is that we all have passions and competencies which make us who we are as people, and those translate into what we do as owners, managers and employees. For business it translates into what the business does or does not do very successfully. People and organizations that find themselves outside of the bubble of what they are passionate about and what they are good at doing simply cannot be successful; there is nothing more basic than that. So let's bring the two together and see what we have.

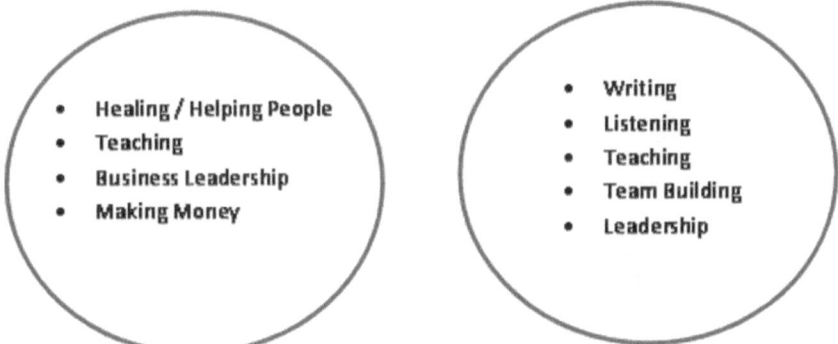

Almost instantly it becomes apparent that there are two areas which are common within the two circles, things which I am both passionate about and am good at. Teaching and Leadership, in other words if I had to pick one thing to do in the world which would be something I enjoyed and was good at it would be teaching leadership or leading a teaching organization. But what if it wasn't quite so smooth and the things in each circle were quite different. At that point it becomes important to define things with a little more detail. For example when it comes to my passion for helping people, we could easily break that down further to "empowering people towards success". Since I have always been a strong believer that a group is far more likely to achieve success than an individual, helping people would definitely involve building teams. The point of this exercise is to get to heart of the matter, not to make it overly complicated or confusing.

Review your two list and look for the areas where your passions and competencies meet. You may need to further evaluate each item to gain a true understanding of what a word means to you. For example if you wrote "teaching" do you enjoy the physical act of imparting knowledge or do like the process of creating the training material? One requires patience, the ability to connect and command respect of peers. The other requires focus, being analytical and methodical. Diving deeper into your passions and competencies can make it easier to see where they overlap.

The Sweet Spot

"Wealth, like happiness, is never attained when sought after directly. It comes as a by-product of providing a useful service."—Henry Ford

Finally, being an ardent capitalist at heart I believe that what we do in our professional lives should be sustainable and hence, generate revenue. Whether a nonprofit working to selfless purposes or hard charging up and coming young millionaires, unless the things we do are able to sustain us financially, we will fail. The number one reason why small businesses go out of business is a lack of capital and financial planning. In other words, they had a great product and/or service which they were passionate about and able to do well but could not generate enough revenue or control the money they made from it. Understand that sometimes what we are passionate about will not make us a sustainable income, however, what we are good at should almost certainly do if applied diligently and correctly. Finances are the core to any business and must always play a key role in determining the way forward. For individuals finances are usually why we go to work every day. We need money to support our families, pay the bills and do activities we enjoy like traveling or watching a show. It is key to keep in mind that the bottom line keeps the vision alive on a practical, everyday basis both at work and at home. With that in mind it is always essential to engage in activities which are financially viable, keeping the passions alive and on the track towards achieving a higher vision.

As a benefit when we are operating in a place where our passions and competencies collide we will be more effective, happier and people will notice. As a manager your team will see your enthusiasm and respond positively. Your boss will view you as engaged and financial benefits will follow. As an organization marrying passions with the competencies of the business and your staff will lead to increased employee and customer satisfaction. Customers, seeing your engagement and belief in what you do will enjoy working with you and continue to do so.

When we take the place where passion and competency meet we are able to create a lasting financially stable situation based on the merging of those two circles and you have arrived at what I like to call the professional sweet spot.

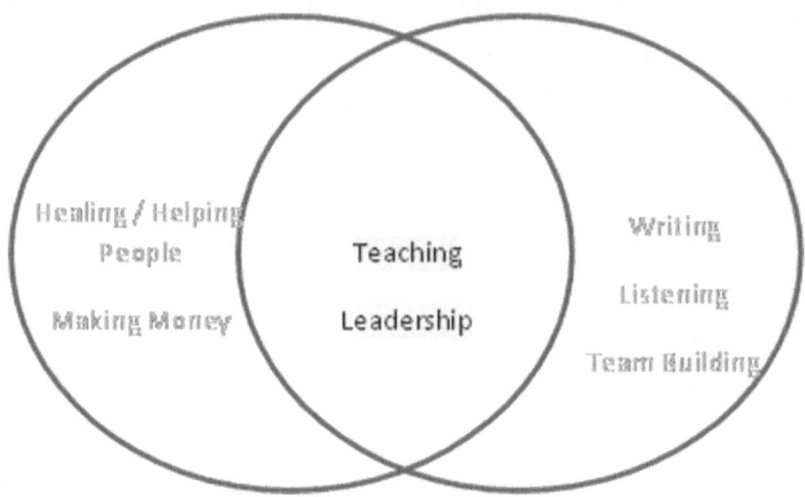

Professional Sweet Spot
- Writing
- Listening
- Team Building
- Healing / Helping People
- Making Money
- Teaching
- Leadership

Now that you have identified your sweet spot are you currently living it in your professional life? Can you think of a time where you had? How did you feel? Were you more satisfied, happier? How was your work performance impacted? You will probably find that these were the times where you felt the best at work and where you enjoyed that aspect of your life.

If I were following this model ten years ago I would have known then that I needed to get into teaching and into a form of leadership. Instead it took me a dozen years of trying to finally identify that there are two areas of my life where I should be focused. What is also important to remember is that just because these two stand out does not mean the rest go away. As I sit here today, it the ability to write that lets me communicate these ideas and the ability to build teams has given me much of my success through the years. Similarly, I hope that through teaching I can help people and empower them to their own success—something I have been fortunate to be a part of for several years in developing a younger generation managers. The point is that all of these play together as long as the sweet spot is the driving factor in choosing a direction.

Using this method with my marketing company we were able to increase our success and overall employee satisfaction. We started out managing data and it evolved into something altogether different. Below is the approach that took it to places far beyond our wildest imagination.

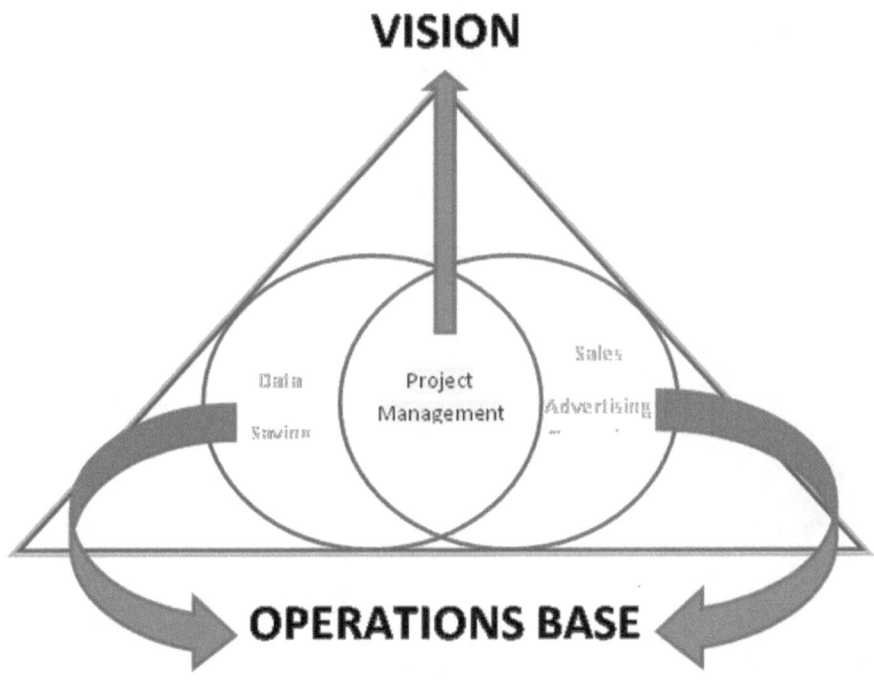

By looking very closely at what we loved to do and what we were extremely good at doing we came to the conclusion that we needed to be involved in project management. This clarity allowed us to create a foundation from where to begin. In this case the base was the two things we were passionate about

- Data
- Saving

Combined with the two things we were specifically competent at

- Sales
- Advertising Campaigns

By focusing on our sweet spot of project management to create a vision for where we wanted to go we created a new entity from the old data management company, one that would go on to manage several high profile advertising and sales events which saved the clients' money and energized our company.

Back to Basics: A Journey Not a Destination

"Always bear in mind that your own resolution to succeed is more important than any other"—Abraham Lincoln

In essence, understanding that when we lose our way, and believe me it is easy to do, the best thing to do is to refocus on what we are passionate about and what we are good at. This is what a successful journey is all about. Over the course of the next few chapters we will discuss a variety of subjects in the context of business and business management, however, each subject is also applicable to personal life. All the incidents are true to my life and all the people are real, making this back to basics journey all about the real world. It has always been my belief that once we truly understand our direction, our vision and establish a firm base of operations we are on the right path. Incorporate the fundamentals, nothing fancy just the basic fundamentals, and success is achievable to anybody who is willing to keep it simple and work hard. Finally, no one can tell you how to define your success, which is a journey you must take of your own accord. This book is a tool to help you identify your elephant and take the first steps in becoming truly successful.

Culture

"No people come into possession of a culture without having paid a heavy price for it."—James A Baldwin

My good friend Saul ran one of the most successful retail outlets in the business. There was little doubt in anyone's mind that Saul was on a fast track to district manager and equally no-one would deny that he had earned it. Saul's shop simply did better year over year and month over month than any store around him. It wasn't location because when the company moved him to a larger, poorly located, store his achievements continued. I have to confess that as a young sales manager I was more than a little envious of Saul's successes, especially when I took over his old store and was a miserable failure at performing the way he could. What boggled my mind were the facts. The facts were that the customers were the same, the store was the same, the merchandise was the same, and even the sales associates were left over's from when Saul managed the store. In all my training I had never come across a situation like this, where I was given all the tools that should have made me successful and simply couldn't. Hungry for answers and determined to get to the bottom of his secret I visited his new store and spent several hours listening and watching his sales team in action. Despite the occasional inclination to brag, Saul himself was a masterful director who kept his team moving and operating at a constant, uncompromising pace. When there was down time from customers they were learning scripts and stacking product at the same rapid stride. I was quite taken considering my own team spent a large portion of their time lounging around or outside smoking. What I couldn't quite understand, then, was how a short paunchy man with a devilish goatee was able to command such a well-oiled machine. That knowledge was not forthcoming and it would be several years before I could duplicate and surpass his accomplishments.

Over the course of many sales classes and an immersion into the world of corporate lingo I had heard often that one needed to create a culture of this or a culture of that, and only by creating a culture would there be true progress. In the sales sense this meant creating a situation where selling was the be all and end all of a person's existence. For the most part, like many people, I snuffed off this idea that somehow there was a culture involved in selling or that culture had anything to do with the profitability of a business. The word culture, to my mind, invoked images of fine dining to classical music and admiring the work of Monet. It wasn't until much later on that I began to research how culture affects companies and it wasn't until I had the opportunity to witness for myself how a culture can form the basis for success in an organization that the idea of a corporate culture began to take a hold. Cultures form a company and ultimately are responsible for how the employees interact, what direction the company takes and finally have a direct and measurable effect on the success or failure of the organization.

The question then becomes what exactly is culture and how does that translate to the young (or old) and rather uninterested worker who has little or no concern with the general welfare of the company as long as the paychecks keep coming? And more importantly how does a great leader take the concept of culture, understand it and implement it in such a way that change becomes inevitable?

On the banks of Lake Washington there is a small deli, run and wholly owned by a middle aged Chinese American lady named Ming. When you wander into her café style deli several things quickly become apparent. First there is no sense of the hustle and bustle one would come to expect in a deli that is so close to some of the most busy and affluent people in the state. The pace visibly slows down as people come in to have a soup or a sandwich and spend their lunch hour chatting amongst themselves or with the deli owners. The next thing you will notice, if you are paying attention, is that Ming and her husband Stan are always directly involved in the preparation of the food and a wonderful smell perpetually wafts out of the kitchen as Ming makes some of the most delicious soups. Stan works the register and the antiquated espresso machine while making small talk with the folks as they hurry in. The place is rustic and quaint with good food served with a side of taking a deep breath. The kids that work at Ming's are usually high school teenagers trying to make some extra money to spend at the local mall, however, what is interesting are that they quickly fall into the pattern of slowing down and enjoying a few moments of the guests time. Even the delivery people tend to stop and have a cup of coffee or spend a few minutes chatting with the owners. In essence when you walk into the door at this small and rather hidden deli you enter a different world, leaving a culture that says "hurry up" for one that says "take a load off and enjoy a few relaxed minutes".

Culture! Dismiss for a second the swirling clouds of unfocused drivel that have become corporate mantras and indeed have so confused the issue that even the guru's themselves really have no idea what they are talking about. Because of it the word culture has just become a catch all for the way an organization thinks, acts and behaves. And while many leaders would like to flatter themselves into believing that they have set the tone that the culture is a reflection of their own vision, most would in fact find that if the cultural mindset among the lower echelons were anything to go on, the leadership should hang their heads in shame. Instead of wandering down the path of wondering how we got to talking about vision, let's instead look at what culture is, how it can be created and most importantly how it can be molded to fit the dreamy vision of management.

Most commonly culture is used to define a set of shared attitudes, values, goals and practices that characterize an institution, organization or group. In other words if it looks like a flock of geese, smells like a flock of geese and poops on your lawn it is probably a flock of geese.

The word culture comes from the Latin word colere, which directly translated means "to cultivate". This then raises the specter that not only can culture be cultivated, but that the culture in most organizations is in fact a culture that has been cultivated through the passage of time. The first time I heard this analogy of culture I began to look around me at the organizations with which I was associated, and if your experiences are anything like mine it is rather sobering when you begin to realize that cultures are not accidental.

Take for example a large and unnamed organization that specializes in delivering letters, postcards and packages. Over the last several decades this organization has become an elite class, only those who meet certain criteria are allowed in. This organization then became bureaucratic because it is so difficult to replace the workers once they are in the door that after a time the management simply stops working on efficiencies and starts focusing on cost cutting as a way to be more profitable. Lines get long, customers get impatient and yet the company refuses to change despite the fact that it is losing massive amounts of market share to younger, fresher and more aggressive organizations and is in imminent danger of becoming obsolete. How in the world did we get from "always on time" to "let's take the clocks out of the waiting area so that the customers aren't aware of the time they are spending here"? The answer is simple—culture.

Culture, if not managed correctly, will (just like your lawn in the spring time) take on a life of its own and pretty soon your will have to use a weed whacker to go find your car. This is the first and most important lesson about culture. If you take nothing else from this chapter, realize that culture of some nature and some pedigree will flourish in your organization. The question is will it be the carefully manicured lawn or a tumble of weeds, dandelions and carpet weed?

I founded a manufacturing and distribution company where I learned this the hard way. Although myself, and others in leadership levels, had visions and ideas for our company culture that is not what developed. Due to some miss-hires a culture started to form like the dandelions on the lawn. It started with one annoying yellow flower and the seeds (like attitudes) spread to all that is around it. Before you know it the entire lawn is peppered with yellow. Then you have a choice to make. Allow the dandelions to become a permanent fixture of your lawn or use weed poison to permanently remove them. At my company I could not allow a culture to continue that was contrary to our vision. Painful as it was I had to remove the team members that carried the contrary attitudes.

Culture happens to us all, deal with it.

Attitude

> *"Attitude is a little thing that makes a big difference"*—Winston Churchill

By definition, culture is a shared attitude. It is the way your work force perceives their life as it pertains to working at your organization and ultimately it is the very thing which will either drive your organization into ruin or cause it to soar. Attitude is everything. Most leaders understand this concept which then leads to a fundamental flaw in thinking which goes something like this "if I have the right attitude, people will naturally follow me and we will all have the right attitude". Wrong, dangerously and sadly, deeply wrong. Remember the old adage about a rotten apple in a crate of apples—now perceive yourself as one great apple in that very same crate. You are the rosiest, shiniest, most succulent apple that ever was destined for Ma's apple pie, but towards the bottom of your crate is another apple. This apple is crusty, has brown spots and quite frankly smells like mold. So let me ask you a question, which apple do you think will have the most influence on this entire crate of fruit?

The good news is a smart operator always has an eye out for the moldy apple whether it is in the form of a person, a behavior or a way of thinking. Every organization has them, which is why it becomes so important to create an atmosphere that encourages the growth of shiny red super stars and discourages a bad attitude from taking hold. Understanding that the combined attitude is what drives a culture is a key note to success. Even more importantly is understanding how to drive the attitude in the right direction.

Some of the most successful organizations in the world believe that if you hire for a great attitude, you can train a person and hone the knowledge that they possess. Knowledge and skill with the wrong attitude can spread the attitude poison throughout the company just as fast as mold in the barrel of fruit.

Leading Cultural Change

> *"Leadership is the art of getting someone else to do something you want done because he wants to do it"*
> —Dwight D Eisenhower

The answer to having a successful culture can be found in the very definition of the word itself. Breaking down the definition a little further one finds that culture is a set of shared goals, values and practices.

This is truly where leadership comes into play and where the great leaders separate themselves from the mediocre ones. An organization that functions on a purely top down structure will quickly find that the culture at the bottom of the pile is far different from that at the top of the pyramid. Some organizations have attempted to flip the pyramid upside down to indicate that the workforce is on top of the world. While the average employee may embrace this philosophy its far from the truth. While valuable, employees only see the aspects of a company that pertain to them making them unable, in larger organizations, to envision and implement an entire culture. The reality is most workers will simply look at culture statements and in their minds eye pass it over because we all know that goals and direction come from above. The goals of a culturally sound organization are ones that the company agrees upon as a unit. While it would be foolish to suggest that every worker be part of the final decision making process when it comes to goal setting for the organization, one will find that the mere idea of inclusion tends to positively change culture.

Leading the cultural charge starts at the very first level of management. Ask the question, where do you see this company going and how do you think we can get there? You will probably find that opinions vary from group to group or even person to person. That's why it is so important to establish, convey and actively implement the company culture.

It really does not matter if you are talking to the CEO or the guy who works part time cleaning the floors, you will inevitably find that both have a similar desires at the end of the day. Both want to provide for their families and at the lifestyle they are accustomed to. The company succeeding is the vehicle that drives that and both will have ideas on how to get there. While it is true that the person mopping the floors has no real say in where the company goes, the mere fact that he or she was included creates a sense of belonging. The sharing of goals to all levels of the organization, the back and forth of information from the lowest to the highest and the understanding that we are indeed still a village based society can go far towards creating a positive and productive culture.

On the flip side of this equation is another positive. Many employees when asked about the direction of the company, goals and the path to success will quickly air their own sense of being unimportant. Remember the vigilant operator is always on the lookout for apples that could taint the entire case, and is not afraid to dig among the weeds to find an attitude or a concern which if left unaddressed will fester and eventually become a part of the larger culture. Asking employees their thoughts on company culture, direction and vision may seem like a tedious task and often you wont enjoy the answers. Not asking the questions, however, is simply not worth the risk. Employees will develop opinions and share them with each other and customers regardless of whether or not you ask. The only difference is your ability to proactively address and change those opinions.

A word of caution, too many managers and owners today have the mistaken belief that organizational success is not something that weighs on the mind of the average worker. Nothing could be further from the truth. It is the front line employee who sees how things could be improved, understands the day to day dynamics of the business and whose livelihood very well could depend upon the success of this organization that will set the culture of the company. As such they can often provide insight based on experiences that management simply does not have. Reports can tell numbers. Surveys can convey opinions but the everyday encounters and interactions of your employees tell a more complete story. No one in the village can or should be ignored.

As a young manger beginning to understand how important culture is to the success of an organization I started to build a team that had one common trait, each of them truly valued the idea of success. Being a sales and services organization, we measured our success in terms of sales and in customer satisfaction. The team at its very core consisted of individuals who personally were extremely committed to both of these ideas. They loved to sell and got a deep personal satisfaction from it and equally they were highly dedicated to providing the highest levels of customer service, again seeming to gain a sense of personal victory in the face of excellent customer satisfaction. Over the course of the next year and despite the fact that my group was one of the youngest around we became the most successful team in the state, winning many accolades and much praise for our achievements. The team relished the recognition and took second place as a personal insult. Without realizing it I had stumbled into a key element of creating a successful culture. People with a unified vision and common direction create a culture of success.

Values

> *"Anything that changes your values changes your behavior"*
> —George A Sheehan

People's values are created at a very young age. At their core these values do not change over time and they are the driving factor in a person's life. Values are things your employees believe in and are an essential part of their lives.

First it must identify what character traits it wants to embrace. In other words what is the absolutely nonnegotiable philosophy that drives the company or group?

Second the company must then seek out and staff itself with people whose inner most values are a reflection of that philosophy. Easier said than done? Yes. I would like to say that this can come at a blink of an eye but it does not. As a manager you have to dive deeper in the interview process than you normally would and it may take you longer to hire the right candidate. Trust me it is worth the extra time and wait. It will pay off dividends in the end. Hiring people that embrace and live the culture you want to create is invaluable.

For my team our motto was simple "nobody leaves without buying something". It was something we drove home relentlessly. We talked about it daily, we pushed each other daily and we chanted it like some insane members of a sales cult. As a result we went through a large amount of turnover, people who could not stomach the culture after a while realized that they were out of place and left. Those that stayed understood in the core of their being that this philosophy was about winning, winning for the company and winning for them personally.

Eventually what was left was a fundamentalist group that did not believe in the word "no".

Because the final group fundamentally shared the vision, the goal and the attitude a culture was born. Careful cultivation and relentless pruning of the bad apples led to uncompromising excellence which was upheld at every level of the organization, to a point where even I was held accountable by those who worked for me. Nobody was left out and nobody was above the shared vision.

Change

It is important to note that adaption of culture is internally affected by two forces. These forces are those that are encouraging change and those that are resistant to change. In order to bring about meaningful cultural development it is important for a leader to understand the dynamics, ideology and pitfalls of change.

We start to look at change and how to manage it effectively so as to have the most promising cultural impact. While doing so there is one note of caution about culture. Culture is a constantly shifting phenomenon which requires that those who seek to influence it also change in tune with the changing circumstances. Leaders who fall into a trap of complacency quickly find that they lose their edge on cultural change and become redundant, a part of the cycle instead of the force guiding it.

Take Saul, the manager who first got me wondering about the success of highly cultured organizations. After a short run as a manager he was promoted into a district manager position where he did extremely well, for a while. Complacency and a sense of accomplishment set in and in due course his district, settled into the middle of the pack where it remained for the better part of a decade. His philosophy as middle management was different from the young, fast paced ideology Saul was able to build in his store and lead. It eventually sucked the life out of this vibrant manger, making him just another cog in the companies stagnant culture.

When Saul first got promoted he approached the position with the same vigor he had as a single store manager. He attempted through meetings and working one on one to transfer the attitude and culture of his previous teams to his entire district. What he encountered were people that were uncomfortable with and refused to change. He continued to work with them, to coach them but in the end they would not change. Instead of removing the "bad apples" from their positions he kept them in place thus continuing the same patterns of mediocrity. By choosing to do so it was impossible for the culture, he worked so hard to create, to take hold. Creating and maintaining a positive and healthy company culture is not always easy and often requires making hard decisions. The question you must ask is, "How important is culture to me?" and "Am I willing to do things that are hard or uncomfortable in order to achieve it?". Then ask yourself what your company or team looks like without you leading and promoting culture. Is it worth the risk not to address it and take steps to change it?

Change

> *"Change is inevitable. Change is constant."*
> —Benjamin Disraeli

Change is as fundamental to life as breathing and equally as important. It is an inevitable consequence of existing that manifests itself in every form and yet it is a fundamental human nature to fight change. We fight aging with rejuvenating skin creams and hair replenishment supplements, we fight organizational change by sticking to the "old is gold" mentality and stubbornly dig in our heels when a change threatens to rock our comfy little boat.

On reading the above quote, my first reaction was to brush it off as a catch all statement that failed to include in its view those of us who embrace change, those of us who are catalysts for change and those of us who, well, simply go with the flow. Then I was challenged to examine my own motivation for change a little deeper and I would challenge you to do the same. There are fundamentally three types of people when it comes to change. Those who are catalysts or creators of change, those who are accepting of change including early adopters and finally there are those who flat out don't want to change and still believe the best way to listen to music is on a cassette player. People usually nod in instant recognition of those in their immediate circle who fall into the first and last category; there are also very distinct individuals, in our sphere, that we recognize as falling into the middle group. What is absolutely paramount to remember however is that every single one of these groups is adverse to and will place some resistance to change.

The third group is actually the easiest of the three to identify because they are usually the ones desperately clinging to their first generation flip phone and speaking with them can often be challenging across the torturous sounds of a dot matrix printer. This group views change with a great deal of suspicion and often a deep seated anxiety that this change will somehow unbalance the very axis of the planet on which they exist. Ironically once you persuade this group to change, they will often embrace the new with the same fervor with which they grasped the old.

My parents are excellent examples of this mentality. For years they hung on to an old pair of Motorola E815 mobile phones, which they had purchased on a recommendation from me when the phone had just come out. When the battery died, they scoured across eBay and found replacements and when the unthinkable happened and one of the phones started to give up on life, they even managed to find a reseller and replaced their old e815 with, yep you guessed it, a new e815. Tending to be an early adopter, with a known addiction to technology, I went through half a dozen phones in the time they kept their Motorola dinosaurs. Eventually I bought my step father a newfangled Motorola, which he instantly fell in love with. It took another year to wean my mother off her old phone and eventually it was a Windows 6 device that finally got her to pack in the clamshell. Incidentally it's been over 3 years since she took over the Windows phone, which is all but obsolete itself and stubbornly refuses to look at anything else.

These are the same people in the office that will complain about retiring a version of the product you manufacture or service package you provide even when the new offering will be better for the customer and company in the long run. The old product or service will always be better than the new even if it is no longer relevant. We all have worked with people like this so it is important to remember that although change to them is like pulling a tooth slowly with string, in the end they will become ardent supporters of the new product or service once comfortable with it.

The second group in the change-gang are the early adopters, people who are quick to embrace change as it comes their way. You will always recognize this group by its seeming enthusiasm when you discuss new ideas and concepts. This group is always ready to try new things, by pure definition they are the ones who take the plunge with a firm belief in things going well. Unfortunately there are two consequences to taking the plunge, depending solely on the condition of the water into which said plunge was taken. There are warm tepid waters which have the group smiling and encouraging others to come on in, and then there are times when the plunge is into the icy and turbulent waters of the North Atlantic. The change is not always easy, but we will come back to that in a little while. So what happens when the change you implemented does not cause instant results which in turn boosts morale and has your early adopters smiling encouragement to those still lagging behind? The majority will quickly turn around and hightail it for the shore. They will go back to the place where they know the temperature is warm and a tropical paradise on the island of "I know this, hence, its safe" awaits. Once you let them leave the water chances of getting them back to embracing the change decreases significantly. What is important for any leader to remember is that while your early adopters jump in first, they are also equally likely to jump out first and it is critical for you to continue to steer them in the right direction while making sure their experience is a good one.

The early adopters at the office will excitedly participate in new campaigns and activities. They will inform customers of new products and services with zest and vigor. They will actively promote prior to fully understanding and they will just as equally be vocal about any negative experience with the change. Knowing this is important because your early adopters have a direct impact on the rest of the team either way. As a manager it is important to make sure the tools and support are in place to ensure an early adopters experience with the change is a success. Launching to quickly is the equivalent of them diving into the ocean without a life vest or boat to swim alongside. They will go out only so far before looking around for support, whether physical or moral. If they don't find it they will panic and head back to shore.

As I mentioned I tend to be an early adopter when it comes to technology especially mobile phones. Equally there is a strong tendency to keep my old phone, just in case I do not like the new one. Over the course of the years I have replaced many mobile phones, only to go back to the old device stored in my bedside table at the first sign of trouble. As a result I was one of the first to switch to a touch screen multimedia handset, and also among the first to discover that I absolutely hated it which resulted in a rapid change back to my old blackberry. When RIM came out with a touch screen device of its own I sat on my heels, unwilling to trust that even blackberry's stellar reputation could pull off operating anything more than an extremely annoying touch screen device. Eventually I wandered off the safe island and experimented with the Storm II, a phone that has become a fixture in my life until I bought the I Phone. As an early adopter I had found myself back on the safe beaches of non-touch screen until a company was able to come up with a safety net (a platform I was familiar with) and tempt me back into the icy waters of change. In a way the change happened on my terms—the way change usually happens.

The last group is the one that will change after it has been proven to work. They just want to see the early adopters swim (or sink) first.

Once they see a limited amount of success they are happy to give it a try. You will find them pensively waiting at the office to see the reports on how new products and services are being received. They will go out of their way to ask an early adopter for updates on new projects, internally debating when to jump in. Since they use the early adopters as a bench mark they don't risk the same degree of failure and simultaneously don't experience quick success. They will however be consistent over time and the easiest to work with. Before engaging this group in the change you are promoting spend time working with the early adopters to determine what additional support should be offered and what needs to be refined. The goal with this group is to keep everything running smoothly.

Words like dynamic, agent of change, and inspirational are words that recruiters and human resource managers like to throw around when searching for a great leader. The majority of entrepreneurs, business leaders and icons of political theater are seen as agents of change, who lead their group to a new culture. And yet one is faced with the fundamental reality of human life, humans are usually opposed to change. The same is true for the dynamic, inspirational change catalyst that you may see looking back at you in the mirror every morning.

Let's think about it like this . . .

Suppose you wake up one morning and on your mad dash to the office find that your significant other decided it would be far less messy to place the coffee pot, your coffee pot, in the upstairs guest bathroom. First reaction? Okay granted that is a silly and rather unlikely example, so let's look at another.

Suppose you show up to work one morning and one of your immediate supervisors decided that your desk should face east for fen shue reasons instead of the way you have had it for the last 4 years. First reaction? I can tell you what mine would be and though I am not a gambling man I would be pretty willing to bet yours would be about the same *"What the heck is this? What a stupid idea?"*

What happened to the catalyst for change? What happened was the idea wasn't yours and you weren't consulted before what you consider to be an idiotic move was made.

Change is good IF and only IF you are part of the process. Like it or not, it does not matter what group your employee falls into, change that is implemented or demanded without their input is change that is neither welcomed nor easily accepted. Catalysts of change like to cause change, they do not like it when change occurs in spite of them and sweeps them along. Early adopters embrace change as long as they feel like they have a say in what direction the current will sweep them, however if the waters are too icy and they have no stake in holding on, Shangri-La awaits on the flip side of change.

Going back to that example if your boss hired an expert in fen shue to go office to office and meet with everyone you would be likely to oblige. You would politely listen, ask questions and make a decision as to which changes you would like made in your office. Once made you would embrace them and tell others how wonderful they are—all because you were part of the decision making process. By simply including you your boss gave you a feeling of ownership vs. feeling a loss of control.

As a manager it is important to actively seek out ways to include your employees in the process of change before typing up the memo that revolutionizes the way things are done. A practical example would be if as a manufacturing company you were planning on coming out with the next generation of a product you could hand out a company survey asking employees what they thought should be improved. Allowing them to give their feedback, whether implemented or not, makes them feel part of the process and gives a sense of ownership.

What about the opponents of change, the employees that will not like anything new regardless of why or how the change took place. Let's go back to the story of my mother and her e815 for a second. The only way I was able to convince her to switch phones was by letting her get used to the windows phone by playing with it. Showing her the features and without pushing her into anything let the phone and her form a bond. When the change came it was sudden and definite. She announced out of the blue one evening "I like that phone, can you get me one?" Similarly opponents of change simply need time. They need to be exposed to new products or ways of doing things and allowed to observe. This is not a group where you want to demand immediate action. They need more time and if you want them on your team, give it to them. The late adopters frustrate many managers but are often the most loyal employees and ardent supporters once they become comfortable with the change.

For the torch bearers of change there is good news and there is bad news. The good news is change happens. By the sheer desire and personality you possess you will make change happen. The bad news is that change will happen with or without you, and often times in spite of you. Learning to accept that change is inevitable can be the first step to being a great agent of change.

Influencing Change

"Yes we can change"—Barak Obama

In 2008 a young and rather inexperienced senator from Illinois swept the United States in an unparalleled swelling of emotion and ultimately won himself a seat behind the grandest desk of all. President Obama's rise was unprecedented in the grand old game of politics. For the purpose of this book, however, the focus is not on the rise of Barak Obama nor about politics and policies—instead is it critical in our time to note that in one simple sentence Obama has forever demonstrated how to motivate change.

Change begins with an idea. An idea that is fundamental to the functioning and integrity of an individual, a company and even a nation. Before we go any further, however, it is essential to note that the change we are discussing is not necessarily monumental change, rather it manifests itself in the everyday mundane tasks which ultimately keep all the cogs working. Change does not have to be political upheaval in Washington D.C., it can just as easily be the adoption of a less authoritative management approach or a switch to cheerios for breakfast. All change begins with a single thought

"This would be so much better if . . ."

People who influence change have become very good at catching those seven little words and encouraging further exploration. Whether the sound is inside your head or from the executive board member who sleeps through most of your meetings, whenever a leader hears those words it is a call to action. It is up to the aware leader to carefully take the idea and plant it in fertile soil, or to establish that the idea has little merit and move on.

Over the course of a variety of management jobs I spent a lot of time thinking I knew it all. Does not sound like anybody you know, right? And what was more for the things I did not know there was usually an official company policy or procedure that ensure we stayed on the company line. As a result most conversations with me about change would go something like this . . .

"This would be so much better if xyz"

"Really? That's a great idea, unfortunately the company frowns upon that kind of innovation so I will be sure to take it up with the board at the next meeting but I wouldn't hold my breath. Thank you for the great idea though"

"This would be so much better if abc"

"You know, you're right. Thing is we don't really have a budget for that right now so I will definitely take it under advisement and get back to you when things ease up a little, ya know?".

And yet, I pride myself with being a change catalyst. In the course of a few seconds I had told these employees that they were simple employees designed to be cogs in the wheel and while I would condescendingly agree that their ideas were okay, nothing would ever come of it so they may as well shut up and go back to work. The unfortunate thing is we all do it.

So here is what I learned to do. When someone would approach me with a change statement I would make sure I had time to listen for a few minutes and let them describe what they were talking about and then ask them to write it down and give me a copy. Initially this got some strange looks until I would explain "I tend to be forgetful when I get busy and I really don't want to waste a great idea because I forgot about it. Also writing it down will let your solidify what you are trying to do and present it much more accurately . . . after I have read it we should talk about it some more, okay?"

Pretty soon an ingenious co-worker came up with a suggestion box and once a week I would pull all the ideas out of the box and read them, evaluate their merit and discuss the ideas (good, bad and indifferent) with my management team. We would also share the ideas and open general meetings for discussion. The number of great ideas that came out of those suggestion box postings and the number of bad ideas which evolved into good ideas during the follow up meetings were more than I could have come up with by myself in an entire lifetime. Remember change comes from an idea like flashes of stupidity or flashes of brilliance which can happen to everyone.

In the case of the 2008 US presidential elections the idea was one of empowerment—in a sense "yes we can" was taking the idea that the American government could be changed because the people were in had the power to make it so. The common man and woman had the ability to change the nations direction with his thoughts, her ideals and their vision for "this would be so much better if . . ." to which Barak Obama responded with "Yes we can" and in so doing won the White House.

The point being that you as a leader can as well, if you are willing to take the steps needed to be an agent of change.

1. Listen: We have already established how easy it is to kill change making ideas. Take the time to listen (or read) what people have to say
2. Write it down: When a great idea happens it is usually unformed and not fully thought out. Writing it down makes a world of difference as you start to dissect it and evaluate implementation.

3. Discuss it openly and freely: If you think an idea stinks say so but do it in a manner that invites further discussion. The thought behind the idea may prove valuable even if the initial suggestion was not.
4. Involve people: Remember its "yes we can", not yes I can while you tag along. Many managers subscribe to the ideology that it is important to tell people what to do, how to do it and why it is important. I differ in one small and critical way—I have come to find that if you involve people in the process they have a strong understanding of what needs to be done, a clear vision for why and very often will help you figure out how. Teams succeed, individuals shine.
5. Implement the ideas fully. It is easy to have lofty ideals and dreams of change, it is quite another to implement these ideas especially in the face of often deeply entrenched opposition. Evaluate your team and their view of change. Categorize them and treat each category differently. You will have far greater success implementing change when you do so.

Listen Learn Change

> "Courage is what it takes to stand up and speak; courage is also what it takes to sit down and listen."—Winston Churchill

Many great managers, like politicians, come in with ideas of change and a great deal of enthusiasm for creating a new culture only to find that things are not always fair winds and sunshine. Buffeted by the lack of support from the never say change folks, desperately trying to keep the early adopters on track and driven to insanity by other change agents who have their own ideas for change many leaders fall prey to their own ego and bring down the iron fist. They stop communicating and discussing their way through the mine fields and quickly take on ideological positions that are both indefensible and bad for business.

For several months I had found myself under immense pressure to bring profitability up. Implementing idea after idea, there was no time for discussion or dissention. My team took most of this in their stride but what I failed to realize is there was a growing sense of rebellion brewing in the ranks and while the team was performing the tasks I asked, the quality of work was slipping, gossip and backbiting were becoming the order of the day and overall I found us getting further behind. Frustrated I expressed my disappointment at a closed staff meeting to my management team and it was then that one of my managers said words I will never forget. She said "We started failing when you stopped listening". Two weeks later I called an all hands team meeting and spent the better part of 3 ½ hours listening as the team hashed out the different ideas and came up with a variety of solutions to my problems. Though, originally slated for about an hour the meeting went on until the team decided that we had reached an answer to each of the challenges. We left that evening with a new sense of purpose and direction for the group. Three months later the team was still holding itself accountable to the changes we had agree to and the unit itself showed double digit performance increase along with taking its first steps into profitability.

There is word of caution for all of us out there who believe we are a driving force of change, have cultivated great habits to empower change, and are a catalyst of change. Rigidity has no place in the change cycle because in order to cause transformation, a leader must be able to be a part of change. As a manager you cannot expect your team to embrace change you put forth no matter how great the idea.

You have to help them understand and embrace change. Look for ways to include them, provide support, set realistic time frames for implementation, allow for observation and listen.

Great leaders understand that change is going to happen and it is important to guide change in the direction you want it to go.

The Team

"Coming together is a beginning. Keeping together is progress. Working together is success."—Henry Ford

Perhaps hardest lesson for a leader to learn is one I like to call the anti-superman lesson in humility. This, while a bitter pill to swallow for those among us who excel at overachieving, is an essential part of leadership. Plus there is an extremely positive side to this learning that; believe it or not, you are definitely not the superhero you try to be.

My anti-superman lesson in humility came while managing a health spa in one of the more prestigious areas of Washington State. During the course of my first few weeks I learned several lessons, most of them challenging.

First I learned that the current staff was cliquish and openly hostile to change. This was not something I had dealt with on a large scale before which meant that my method of dealing definitely left much to be desired. Then came an education from the customers who expected the service to be the kind of ego boosting pampering they had come to count as the norm from the ownership team. As a third lump, operationally the place was a mess, ranging from rooms physically being full of junk to processes that had not been updated since the Stone Age. And finally the fourth lesson came from the owner himself who was happy to be hands off while having me clean up the mess. When all these were combined it did not paint a pretty picture; leaving me to quickly don my superman costume and set to work fixing it all.

It was then that I was taught some of the hardest and most critical lessons of my career. These lessons quickly converged and in so doing made my life a living hell for several weeks.

The Lessons

After donning my superman cape I did what all true superheroes tend to do—charge straight ahead and leap jump or fly. The problem is I am not actually superman and for us normal mortals pausing to evaluate the situation before leaping is generally a good idea. In typical hard charging fashion I proceeded to immediately address and change all of the issues at once from which came three major lessons, some frustration and many long hours for me.

Lesson one was never fire your entire frontline crew before taking the time to hire and train new staff. Regardless of how incompetent a team member may be the fact that they have the ability to fog up a mirror by breathing on it saves you from having to work 88 hours a week. It is much harder to find the time to hire and train the staff you want when you are filling the holes left by the staff you just fired.

Lesson number two never make the customer mad until you are the subject matter expert and are willing to provide a customer friendly solution to their quest for endless perfection. Understand that decorum and finesse are much better solutions then fist and aggression. Customers like employees don't want change so taking your time will ensure that you don't lose your customers, and the company's revenue stream along the way.

Third, address the operations only once you have a working team in place that will follow what you are implementing and believe in progress. If your team is not yet loyal to you, mistrust you or you are in the middle of major hiring and/or firing shifts the chances of the team going along with operational changes is slim to none. As we have discussed people are adverse to change and too much at once will leave you with a team that lacks confidence in you as a manager and the organization as a whole. Take care of your employees first. Get the team in place then introduce the operational changes you want. You will spend less time in frustration and the team will be more energized to tackle new challenges.

Finally, if the previous boss wants out in a hurry, chances are there's a very good reason for it. Do not be surprised to be walking into a mess or challenges greater than you were told. In a new position you have a unique opportunity to mold a team. Your efforts spent at the beginning will be well worth it in the end.

My lack of pause and quickly charging ahead left me with a skeleton crew, none of the support I needed, angry customers and disgruntled owners. While that did not last long it could have easily been avoided all together. When a leader gets into a new position or takes over a new department it is easy to charge in, create a whirlwind of change and often the person most impacted is the leader themselves.

The reason I tell this story is to emphasize one key point. No one, no matter how brilliant or talented, can run an organization, a department or a section of the business all by themselves. The only exceptions are one man shows which are fundamentally designed to be run by a single individual. Every leader goes through a crisis where they feel like the only way to get things done right is to do it themselves and virtually every leader will bite off more than they can chew. While a natural thing to do it prevents you from doing something more productive: team building.

Character of the Team

It is my fundamental belief that, second only to culture building, the most important thing a manager of any acclaim can do is build a strong and well balanced team. The benefits of a strong team are self-evident and the workings of a strong team are clearly demonstrated in the productivity of the team itself. Teams just by sheer man power can achieve in excess over individuals working alone. Great teams can not only produce more in quantity but also quality. Working together individuals will focus on their strengths (passions and competencies discussed previously) and assign tasks they are not good at to others on the team that are. So let us talk about teams.

A team will always, and without fail take on the characteristics of its leader. And like most small children it will pick up on your flaws first in an effort to imitate them. If you have the habit of pensively sticking a pen behind your ear I guarantee that in the not too distant future you will see one or more of your direct reports doing the same thing subconsciously. Because the team has many eyes and ears to your own single set, it becomes critical to set the right tone and message about yourself. High performance leaders lead at all times, regardless of anyone watching. A leader who will only accept exceptional performance of him or herself quickly sends a message to their team that the only acceptable performance is excellence, and the team will respond with pushing itself toward excellence.

A strong team requires herding, much like ducks or cats. Simply by virtue of the fact that high performing teams are usually made up of high performing individuals there will always be a tendency to wander off the beaten path and explore the unknown. Even teams made up of consistently diligent people will still develop ideas and procedures that can be unproductive for the business. Teams are made up of people, each person bringing their history, ideas and attitudes to the table on a daily basis. Good leadership requires a constant eye on the team to ensure that what is brought into work is what is needed to be consistent with the culture you are developing and goals that have been set. It is up to the leader of the group to ensure that the focus of the group remains on the ultimate goal, adjusting that goal as needed.

Clear Goal Setting

Teams that win understand the goal and accept it as an inherent part of their day. Too often goals are lofty ideals that managers strive to meet, rather than part of the everyday grind of a single team member. Ask the lady counting linen on an assembly line what the big picture is and you will get her picture, and her goal which will often be a far cry from the goals of the leadership. Ask a mid-level manager what their goals are and it will likely be based on a widget specifically having to do with their team. As the CFO what his goals are and it will likely involve profitability margins and expense control. The CEO will have a goal relevant to the overall health and performance of the company but will probably not know what the mid-level managers goal is or the woman on the assembly line. Unless owners take active steps to clearly communicate company goals and vision the employees that make up your work force wont understand it and implementation will be from luck not purpose. Management needs to ensure that employees understand how their individual goals play into the big picture of what the company is trying to accomplish. Without that understanding you will have a disjointed team that often works against each other rather than with each other.

When the team understands the vision of the leadership and clearly sees their contribution to the bigger picture the results are teams that pull together. If you have ever watched dog sled racing in Alaska, that is by far the best example of how a team works towards a goal. While the lead dog sets the pace and the human sets the direction every dog on the team knows that they must pull their weight in order for the sled to fly forward to the goal. Somebody stops pulling and everyone slows down together.

Communicate Till It Hurts

Communication is the key and strong teams demand it. Caught up in the humdrum of every day working life we tend to communicate on a very basic level. The stronger the team the more demanding the requirements of communication from the leader of that group. Going back to my experience from earlier, as I built a performance driven team they came to demand statistics, numbers and operational efficiency reports on a daily basis. This team expected to be kept in the loop, after all they were the ones achieving the results and it behooves a good manager to be willing and able to keep up with the demands of a highly communicative team.

When demanding more of your employees remember to take the time to share success with them. Managers that expect success often forget to take the small moments to communicate. The simple act of handing out a report showing positive progress, or publically acknowledging improvement can make a big difference. At this stage you have cultivated a team that admires, respects and trust you. If they didn't they would not work so hard to be a success. As such most will look for some sort of affirmation from you. Make it sincere, descriptive yet brief. There is no need to flatter but a sincere congratulations goes a long way toward a team feeling appreciated.

Self-Accountability

The best teams quickly become self-aware and this leads to an outstanding level of accountability. Teams that gel and work well together will also hold each other accountable to the standards and goals which are set by the leader. A team that holds itself accountable is a delight to work with. Rather than being a babysitter manager you can become a coach, helping your team and each member achieve greater results by harnessing their skills.

As communication remains open and there is no ambiguity this team will also self-motivate and self-train when new members come aboard. The team, having come to expect success, will often have zero tolerance for continued bad performance of new members making it obvious when someone is not a good fit. When you have an established culture and team in place it is important as a manager to listen to the feedback you get from your team. Teams that practice self-accountability are an asset but you must show your confidence in them and their judgment for it to continue long term.

Great teams however are functionally useless unless they have the right kind of leadership. There are four primary types of leadership styles we will deal with in this book, simply because there are a million leadership models and a gazillion leadership styles none of which will fit into a book focused on the basics

Leadership Styles

Leader Number One—The Alpha: The hard charging get it done driver who is relentless in his/her pursuit of victory. These leaders are quick to identify because they do everything with purpose and momentum. Constantly moving quickly so as not to waste time in getting from point A to point B, they are always on the go and, hence have very little time to develop exceptional people skills. Recognizing an alpha leader is never hard. They are the ones who are moving at a hundred miles per hour, have jumped three stages ahead of the conversation, and will be impatiently tapping their foot waiting for the rest of the world to catch up.

Pros: This leader will build a team that is strong willed and aggressive. The alpha will stay in control of the group and will have no problem with burning out the weak links. Victory in the form of achievement and excellence are the only acceptable results for the alpha who sees second best as the first looser.

Cons: Impatient to a flaw this leader makes no bones about running rough shod over an employee to get the job done. This leader can often be a lousy communicator. I mean, who has time for telling you the details which you really don't need to know right?

Leader Number Two—The Analyst: The data, facts and figures guy who needs a spreadsheet for everything. Again not a hard leader to identify because they talk the way they think in facts and statistics. Ask an analyst about sales gains and you are likely to get statistics from the last several years. Slower and more deliberate than the Alpha, the Analyst tends to be a perfectionist who believes that the devil is definitely in the details. If you need to recognize an analyst look for someone who when you ask them a question will lean back in his or her chair and meditatively contemplate the ceiling, or rapidly open up a number of spreadsheets to give you accurate information. Analytical leaders are bothered by quick solutions or glib responses, taking the time to let you know why there is no such thing as a quick fix.

Pros: Teams built by the analyst will be a highly efficient team at producing the highest quality of goods/service. Analysts tend to hire other analysts because of the way they communicate which can be a good thing. Customers love the extra attention to detail and there are very few errors in their work, since short cuts are not an option.

Cons: An extremely analytical team will drive you, and the customers, absolutely nuts. An analytical leader will tend to be overly critical and slow to make decisions, often leading to a log jam of stuff which just needs to get done. An analytical leader can spend much of his or her time "getting back to you", which can be frustrating in a pinch and can feel like a lack of leadership.

Leader Number Three—The In Touch Leader: This is a leader who leads by the emotion, guided by feelings and will be the one who spends time getting to know his/her team members personally. The In Touch leader will tend to want to discuss things and reach consensus rather than bark orders. They tend to be excellent team builders because they are easy to work for besides having a genuine empathy towards team members and customers. This leader is also not hard to identify if you know what to look for. The in touch leader will always have make time for you to air your frustrations, talk about the weather, or discuss the latest episode of "Desperate Housewives". They do this, not because they are interested or have nothing better to do, but because they believe that if they don't listen your feelings might get hurt and that team members that know you care are happier and more loyal.

Pros: The In Touch leader will have a very harmonious team that plays well together and brings in that "family" feeling. Customer satisfaction will be at an all time high because of the high levels of empathy oozing from this team. Doing it in a way that makes everybody happy is definitely a motto to live by.

Cons: The empathetic management style can tend to get stale after a while and cause employees to take advantage of the listening ear they are used to. It will also not play well with the previous two leaders, making it hard to have a multifaceted team. This management style also makes it difficult to eliminate employees that do not fit with the culture or team you are trying to build.

Leader Number Four—The Chameleon: Perhaps the most common and yet the hardest leader to spot is the chameleon. The chameleon does not really have a leadership style and will adapt his / her style to one of the other three depending on the situation. The chameleon really had one primary goal, do enough to fly under the radar without being caught and exposed.

As mentioned chameleon leaders can be among the hardest to spot, however, there are ways of identifying these leaders by knowing the other three styles. Organizations that have quick turn over of teams where the team members are often left feeling disoriented and unsure of the expectations are usually lead by chameleon managers. Out of necessity, having not discovered a comfortable style of their own, these leaders will swing to wild extremes ranging from the ramping Alpha to the most empathetic In Touch leader. This bewilders teams who quickly emulate their leader and ultimately are bad for business because customers do not want to deal with a schizophrenic team.

There are good chameleon leaders and bad chameleon leaders though I tend to call the good chameleon leaders versatile. Versatility in leadership is one of the key survival mechanisms and regardless of a primary style, great leaders quickly learn to be versatile and communicate as the situation requires. They have come to understand that teams consist of all kinds of people and adapt their delivery and style to match the person whom they find in front of them. You want versatility in leadership.

Chameleon on the other hand are cancerous because they grow and develop teams that produce just enough to not get slapped but ultimately are a slow bleed on great customer experience and overall company productivity. Sadly, as I mentioned earlier, this is the most common form of manager out there. And consequently this is also the most common working team out there as well.

Effects of the Team

It is critical to remember that people when put in teams, and placed correctly, work together as a pride of lions. Feasting when there is plenty, hunting when needed, and laying around in the shade as much as possible. When the correct culture is put into place this pride of lions turns into a herd of veritable elephants, spending their time moving ever forward under the guidance of the matriarch. Just as a herd of elephants quickly overcomes virtually any obstacle and works in tandem to ensure the success of the herd, so too will an effective team take on any challenge, circle the wagons when they need to, and ultimate feast on the lushest of feeding grounds.

In a final note on teams, strong teams will stay together long after the primary uniting factor has long since faded. Some of the teams I worked with years ago are still very close, hanging out together in their spare time and reminiscing about the times when they all worked for a common cause. The culture we created was so strong that it formed a timeless bond which transcended the work place and to all intents and purposes bonded these individuals into a family like unit, which I have no doubt will continue to stand the test of time. Even more impressive is the fact that the lessons the team learned together still forms a nuclear part of who they are and is never far from their behavior when they are together. It becomes so deeply engrained in the team psychology that the members carry that culture with them and attempt to change the place they find themselves now, sometimes successfully and sometimes not. This kind of devotion to the culture is the highest praise any manager could ever ask for.

Advancing Competence

"Work is accomplished by those employees who have not yet reached their level of incompetence"—Laurence J. Peter

Perhaps the most interesting principle I came to read during the course of my career was the Peter Principle, which states that an individual will rise to their own level of incompetence. This principle follows that in a mature bureaucracy people will be promoted continually until they reach a position where they are no longer efficient, at which point they will stagnate. It does not take brilliance to look around and witness the Peter Principle in effect across most of the corporate world, and indeed the world at large.

The Peter Principle

Formulated in 1969 by Dr. Laurence Peter and Raymond Hull, the principle focuses on an employee being promoted based on their competence at their current job and not necessarily on the core requirements of the job into which they are being placed. Promotion based on this principal leads to many people in management positions that simply do not have the skill set necessary for that particular position. When this happens over time it will be those in lower positions, and have not yet reached their level of incompetency, that drive the organization forward. Ultimately, however, this can cause losses in productivity and direction for the company because the "leaders"/

managers will not be able to set the tone and pace of a company's performance, not for a lack of desire but for a lack of skill. The Peter Principle (PP) follows the following organizational structure

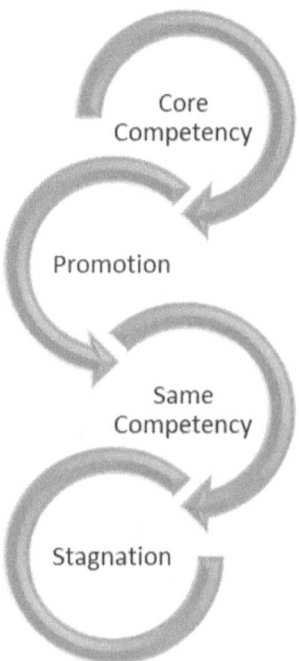

What then can one do to avoid this situation without constantly bringing in new faces? Constant renewal of the work force often causes a great deal of angst among employees who, doing a good job, have come to expect to take the next step in the corporate ladder of success.

When hiring, even at the very baseline, virtually every company fails to set a clear and defined career path for their new hires. Look around, talk to a neighbor or your colleague in the cubical next to you and ask this simple question "What does your career path look like?" I guarantee that you will get a blank look, a shrug or a vague answer that includes elements of their own personal desires and goals. Even better, if you are a manager of any level, pick a staff member at random and ask them to explain the career path you have set for them—if you are able to get a clear vision from this critical member of your team, then you have successfully planted them on the road to success. Chances are, however, you will get the same blank stare, shrug or vague meandering answer. To business owners, managers and shareholders this lack of direction in every level of the company you are associated with should terrify you. It merely means that your employees will and have been following the Peter Principle.

Career Trees and Paths

"Let the path be open to talent."—Napoleon Bonaparte

The reason we prefer to call career planning a tree instead of a path is purely metaphorical. A path may stretch out for miles, splitting and coming to cross roads sometimes but mostly just a long road to nowhere. As an exercise draw a path without any specific direction, have those around you do the same. Very often what you will get is a series of lines on a page, wandering aimlessly or squiggles that go in circles. Very rarely will you get an artist in the bunch will draw a superhighway of roads leading in different directions and taking you to different places. Now, if you were to treat these squiggles on the page as a road map to the future, you would have either one long boring signpost after another down a dust covered path or a track that doubles back and really never gets anywhere. Both of these are worn thin by those who went before and dotted with little white crosses along the side of the road where careers died. Morbid? The sad fact is career paths are morbid for many employees, especially those who have never been coached or counseled into having higher expectations. Then have the same group draw a tree, and you already know you will get a great deal of diversity. From bushy trees with no clear definition, to fancy palm trees, to scantily covered branches, and even trees with apples on them, you will see a spectrum of difference. Trees are in essence a definition of life, finding their beginnings in a tiny seed and growing large and lush. Trees are also not a single unit lonely along a path way that leads nowhere, instead they are a vibrant organism where each leaf, each branch, and each root plays a key role in the overall survival of the tree and its growth. Trees have many branches allowing for a variety of talents and strengths to be used, and serve as an excellent pictorial view of a thriving company. A tree versus road, the idea is the same as long as there is some level of planning, preparation and consideration put into every employee's future with you.

Whether a path or a tree, career planning cannot be something that you do for your employees. It must be something you do with your employees. In order to be successful it requires a level of insight that you simply will not have into the core motivations, hopes and dreams of your team. You may think they are good at sales so naturally they would want to advance into sales management. The reality may be far from that. The same person that is good at sales may find management boring but gets excited at the idea of training other people to sell well. Communication and open dialogue are key to successfully creating career paths with each employee that works for you. For your employees having a plan will keep them more engaged and committed to staying with the company long term. For you employee retention and engagement will lead to a more successful and operationally sound company and team.

Another mistake that many companies make is a lack of succession planning with regard to each of the positions within the organization. It is often not understood what the core competencies are for various positions and what each employee is responsible for. Even companies that do have a job description for their structure tend to make it dry, unreadable and in due course do not use it when promoting or seeking to hire for a specific area of expertise. The first step therefore is to understand what a job core competency looks like and how to match the right person with the right career tree. This should be done often as a company is a living thing that changes constantly. Every position within the organization should be evaluated and a determination made of who within the organization could step into this position if needed. If the answer is no one you need to decide whether or not you want to train someone and increase their skill sets or hire from outside. Although no manager wants to think about an exceptional team member leaving the company, this is life and it happens. People will leave and people will get promoted. The important thing is to be prepared in case they do. Not taking the time to analyze each position and ask these important questions leaves you exposed to the operational risk of losing a good employee without a plan or replacement.

Organizational Structure

A successful organization starts with an organizational chart, as the room takes a collective and horrified gasp, which clearly defines the structure and hierarchy of the organization. Over the last few decades we, as a corporate world, have gotten caught up in a sense of feel good management, which revolts at the idea of such an archaic concept as a written and defined organization chart. The idea that people need to know where they stand in an organization has been vilified as though the employee is simply not smart enough to count just how many people are above or below their position. For clarity sake it is important to understand that an organizational chart has been misrepresented as a symbol of power and a pinpointing of where people stand in the food chain. It is, in fact, a much more positive tool whose key function should be to graphically represent where someone could be going and just how far they can climb with the proper road map. For a chart to clearly define this it must start at the very bottom (or very top if you prefer upside down charts) and show a clear and distinctive path way all the way to the top (or bottom). In other words it must represent a planned journey for every individual in the organization.

When writing an organizational structure chart there are a few clear guidelines that must be followed in order to a. Make it successful and b. Make it a growth tool. These are.

1. Start at the bottom of the chart with the entry level employees and work your way to the top
2. Use specific titles to define specific job functions. Often titles can be misleading because of their inflated sense of importance or underinflated sense of priority. If a position is in a management role, call the position a manager of *specific function*.
3. Avoid using names, even though certain positions are already filled. This will create a sense of organization not hierarchy.
4. Understand that this is a living document, much like a tree, which will change and be modified as times change and the company's direction is altered.
5. Remember that no tree can survive without a strong, deep root system which is its core management.

A wonderful way to get an understanding of how the company is perceived is to get employees to draw the organizational chart as they see it. Keeping in mind that for each individual, their own perception is the reality in which they live, finding out what the world looks like through their glasses is a critical component to understanding the motivation and communication levels in a company. Another key to remember is that every person has an idea of how they would like the chart to be structured. It is never a bad thing to know what an "ideal career path" would be for an employee, reminding them that this is the real world and no one makes it to CEO without years of hard work.

Examples of organizational charts are:

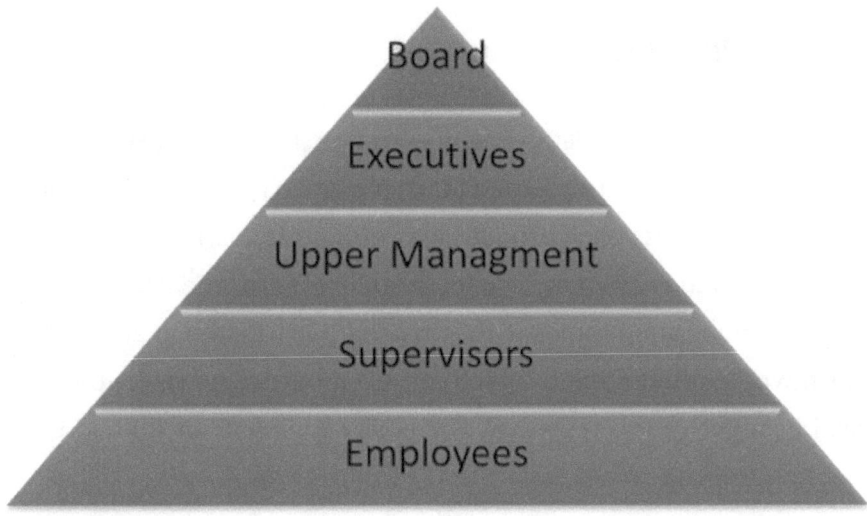

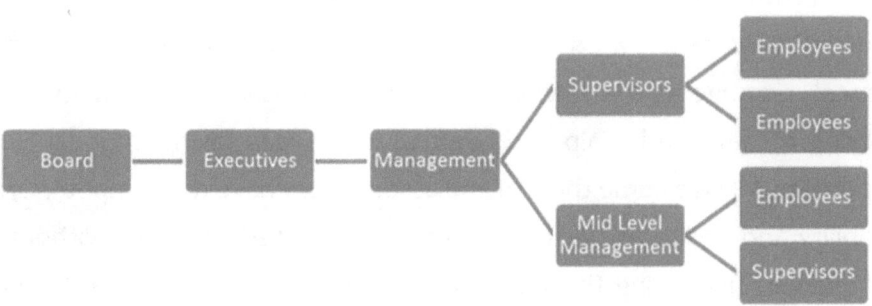

At this point, you have a defined organizational chart which shows any and every employee the steps to becoming the leader at your particular organization, whether companywide or in the group you manage. Now comes the fun part where each of the jobs listed on the tree have to be giving core competencies and behavior identifiers.

Core Competency

When I joined the military many years ago, I had great expectations of the thing that the army would teach me when I got to basic training. Other than the discipline aspect I was excited to learn how to march in synch with the rest of my squad, shoot like a pro, and use the battle field communication radios. Never having participated in any activity which would require me to march or use a battlefield radio, the only skill I brought to the table was the ability to shoot since I had been shooting from age nine.

Imagine my shock when on the first day of pre-boot camp we were expected to march in tune and keep in step. No one shared the commands or told us what we were expected to do when orders were barked out, rather it seemed like the instructors believed we were born with the innate knowledge of what to do at the command of "half left face". Strange as this might seem, this is precisely the mentality we bring to new leadership and even to employees taking over a new position. We welcome them in and assume they have the competency, ability and desire to perform all that is expected of them. Without, however, first doing this exercise we ourselves may not even know what competencies they need to have let alone if they possess them.

For purpose of clarity a core competency is a skill or trait which is typically a skill they are naturally good at or have learned or achieved during an individual's career and/or life. Identifying the core competencies needed for a position can be easy but don't rush as it requires reflection. For example in my current position of CEO I have the priviledge of being involved in all areas of our manufacturing and distribution company. When working with managers, recruiters and Human Resources on hiring I have discovered something. It is easy to identify the obvious traits yet very often character traits are missed. Here are some examples:

- Competencies needed for Sales Associates:
- Self-Motivated
- Diligent
- Personable/Friendly

*These are all things which are easily identified through observation and can be easily judged during an interview process. What is equally, if not more important, is a single and often missed skill:

- Tough-Mindedness

Without it a sales person will not succeed.

Bookkeeper:
- Detail oriented
- Analytical
- Responsive

*Again all of these competencies are easy to identify. What is easy to miss?

- Good Communicator

This ability does not typically come up when discussing this position. However if they do not have it when questions about accounts arise or a process is not working or they are unsure how to handle a certain payable or receivable they may not ask you. Trust me when I say it is dangerous to have a poor communicator in this position.

You can see the importance of taking your time when analyzing the core competencies needed for each position in your company or group. Review the interactions you have had with employees in these positions, both positive and negative. Think about how they need to interact with customers or other employees on a daily basis. Be thorough.

While this may seem slightly challenging at first, one must remember that a competency is a single word or phrase that may be defined in one sentence or less. In order to keep it simple it is essential that competencies are clearly defined in the simplest possible terms. An example would be

Time Management: A range of skills, tools and techniques used to manage time when accomplishing specific tasks, projects, and goals.

So now the Org Tree for each position starts to develop leaves. Each position is going to have at least three core competencies which are absolutely critical to the position itself. By clearly defining these three skills one will find that many of the junior employees seeking to rise to the next level will self-eliminate because they are not ready, by way of not having fully developed the three skills necessary to efficiently perform the job. In order to build a culture that promotes from within, and give the determined employee goals to shoot for, with each position you must also have three advancing competencies. These are three primary skills for the next position up—which must be achieved in order to be considered for promotion or advancement. This gets a little complicated so bear with me. In graphical form this would look like this

Back to Basics

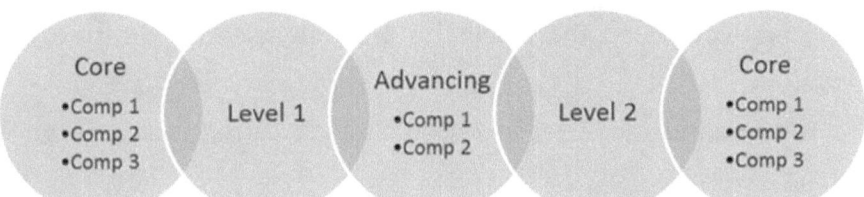

Competencies for Advancement

The third and equally important ingredient to a successful promotion is that an employee brings three core competencies with them, which is one of the main reasons they are being promoted in the first place. These may be referred to as retained competencies. Often skills which are used in one position get the employee placed in a different position only to be swallowed up and forgotten by the demands of the new placement. A timeless example of this is the skill known as effective time management. While many early employees create great habits like list making and keeping of a consistent calendar, once placed into a different position tend to forget these highly effective habits and find themselves drowning in mire of too much to do and too little time to accomplish everything. Time management, like coaching, is often an assumed skill and while it frequently finds itself on job availability postings, it is rarely a skill which employers inspect and promote once an employee starts to climb the corporate ladder.

Let's review: In order to receive a position within your company or group a candidate, internal or external, must have three core competencies to fulfill the job. They must then develop and demonstrate three advancing competencies for the next position, their advancing competencies which will translate into the core competencies of the next position. I like to call these blended competencies. Once moved into the next position the employee must continue to maintain their blended competencies, clearly demonstrate the core competencies, and start to develop the advancing competencies for the next big move.

This requires employees to build on their current skill sets while honing new skills.

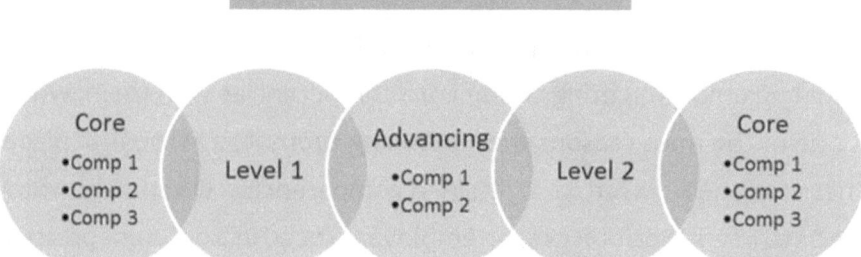

Demonstrating this to employees gives them increased clarity regarding their current position and chunks out smaller steps in accomplishing their career goals. As a manager or owner you benefit by gaining more well-rounded and skilled employees for your organization.

Behavioral Identifiers

A key to avoiding the Peter Principle is to use what are called behavioral identifiers. These are job specific behaviors which an individual must develop and demonstrate before being considered for a position. These behaviors are not something that are published to the organization at large, and indeed it would be counterproductive do as the tendency of naturally aggressive individuals to emulate those behaviors in order to secure advancement. Instead they are maintained within the smallest circle of management as a way to evaluate candidates in light of the position and its requirements. What then, does a behavior and its identifier look like? An easily recognizable example of a position behavioral identifier is found with the president of a country whom we require to be "presidential". There is no clear definition of what being presidential looks like, since it is subjective; however, we all know presidential when we see it—cool, in control, suave, determined, and a hundred other words all of which are required of a president. In your organization it might be that Corporate Sales VP need to be polished or that the HR Manager needs to be soft. These are words that have meaning and can be defined only by your management team as they are specific to you and your business.

Having a clear idea of what behaviors to look for is a key to fitting the right person with the right position. And while it is not essential to do this, I would strongly encourage looking beyond your employees immediate position to one or two positions above them to see if the candidate in question has some or all of the behavioral identifiers to potentially fill those roles in the future. This will help you identify what they need to work on or whether they are at the peak of their personal capacity for advancement.

So now you have a clear career path drawn up, which anybody within the organization can follow because it includes clear ideas of what the expectations are. You also have a clear picture of the competencies required to make the wheels of the engine turn and you know what behavioral indicators to look for when placing or replacing a team member. There are three final steps involved in avoiding an employee becoming trapped by the Peter Principle, collectively known

as Successful Position Management or SPM for short. SPM consists of taking three very deliberate and clear steps which are:
1. Talking an employee into a position
2. Talking an employee through a position
3. Talking an employee out of a position

Talking an employee into a position

Regardless of it being an old professional or a green eared rookie taking up a new position it is absolutely critical that these employees be given the opportunity to be successful. The key to doing this is preparing a talk in session setting a clear and concise idea of the what the job entails before the employee ever sets foot on the job. Some areas that make sense to go over are:
- Key areas of responsibility: What the team member is going to be doing
- Importance to the team as a whole: Why the team member is going to be doing it
- The job itself: How the team member is going to be performing it
- Key Metrics: Performance and what is used to measure it
- Team Members: Who's who and who to look for when you need help.

Much of this seems fundamental, but ask yourself this—"When was the last time I talked an employee into place?"

Talking an employee through a position

The second step to SPM is talking a team member through their position which involves using brief coaching sessions, regular performance reviews and critical connections.

Brief coaching sessions are events that happen on the fly from supervisors, peers and even direct reports. Every successful organization has developed over the years a culture where coaching is welcomed from every direction. These sessions are not critical of performance rather are designed as conversations which can highlight good, bad or indifferent results. An important point to remember is it is okay to talk about the bad stuff. Employees appreciate being told what they are not doing quite right, if you follow up with teaching them how to do it better. Employees with the right behavioral indicators and core competencies will grasp quickly onto these coaching session to identify areas of personal improvement, which will in turn make them much stronger team members. They will use these sessions to gain "nuggets" or tips that can help them be more successful.

Regular performance review which are much more formalized and specifically designed to give and get feedback on employee performance are essential to the growth and development of team members. Set up by supervisors these are structured, time bound and specific to the job. A review is not always a trigger for a raise, something that should be made very clear to employees early on, however, they are an opportunity to praise great behavior, modify behavior that needs improvement and eliminate unproductive or unhealthy habits before they become behaviors. There are a many excellent books written on performance management which describe what outstanding performance reviews look like.

The third and often most neglected stage of the talking through is an active interest in connecting team members with—each other. Often the simplest answers and most profound revelations can be found within a peer group and it behooves good leaders to ensure that as an employee progresses in a position they are well connected to the spider web of people who can make life easier. This ultimately leads to a much healthier work environment and avoids a situation where the "boss" is the only one with all the answers.

Talking an employee out of a position

Finally SPM has a talking out of position. This is when a team member moves to a different position and is especially essential when they are taking on a role supervisory to their current job. Talking out is a two phase process.

The employee talks in their replacement. It is unlikely that anybody is more familiar with a position than the person vacating it, and by making sure that the outgoing employee connects with the incoming employee, teams grow much stronger. This gives the incoming team member a real opportunity to understand the role, get connected and seamlessly assume the responsibilities. It also allows the outgoing team member the opportunity, and prestige of coaching in a new face.

The second stage is a supervisor talk out which involves the outgoing team member and their supervisor. Many people have trouble letting go of positions, especially if they have fulfilled the role for considerable amounts of time. When this talk out takes place it is not focus on their new position, rather it is for the supervisor and outgoing employee to talk about the challenges, accomplishments and memorable moments for the outgoing employee. It is an opportunity for the team member to leave feeling good about themselves and the work they accomplished. Secondarily, it also helps the supervisor be intimately aware of challenges and goals which the incoming employee will need to be coached and trained on.

SPM is about managing the heart of the position, not just the logistics. It creates a sense of belonging and more importantly a clear and stated purpose which in turn speaks to employee retention, successful business operations and a much simplified life for roots of the tree.

Much of what was covered in this chapter is quintessentially basic knowledge. Knowledge that it is so basic in fact that it is often overlooked or forgotten when not written down and implemented day in and day out.

As the famous Greek historian Plutarch stated

"Forgetfulness transforms every occurrence into a non-occurrence".

Companies are not foiled by what they do, rather they are confounded by the things which they do not do. In order to build strong and sustainable teams having the right model in place is extremely important, knowing how to fill positions on that model is even more vital. When the right people are in the right place, driven by a correct culture, and working together as a team there is virtually nothing this team cannot and will not accomplish.

Leadership

> *"Leadership is the art of getting someone else to do something you want done because he wants to do it."*
> —Dwight D. Eisenhower

As we approach the subject of leadership I find myself in a place that is rife with extremes. On the one hand there is a profound sense of humbleness, brought on by an understanding that under the banner of leadership stands a pantheon of great people who have blazed the trail of leadership before me. On the other hand all you have to do to find a book on leadership is walk into a book store and throw your debit card. Considering this influx of training on leadership it becomes much easier for those with little to no leadership ability to learn about it yet still difficult for them to become great leaders themselves. Keeping that in mind and mindful that my own journey in leadership will always grow and increase this chapter will focus on three specific areas that I believe are critical to key leadership.

A man I consider to be one of my business mentors taught me a very important lesson in hiring the right kind of leadership. Having started his own business during his second year of college and successfully running one of the fastest growing hardware providers in India, Raj was looking to add a key individual to his management team. We had recently become friends, having orchestrated an important event for him, I was invited to attend the interviews because he felt I could learn from seeing what kind of management talent walked in the doors. As a young business owner I jumped at the opportunity to see someone who had decades of experience in action. It would be inaccurate to say that anything outside of the ordinary happened during that day, with one exception. While interviewing for lower level positions Raj tended to look for education, experience and stability. However when it came to management especially the key management position he was looking to fill Raj would take a whole different outlook on the hire. While he still looked at the experience and the education, I noticed that he moved through these categories rather quickly and on to a simple question. He would ask "What can you do for me that my team cannot already do?" This it seemed was where many of the recent graduates and even some of the grizzled veterans were caught scratching their heads. Standard answers and well-rehearsed platitudes were dismissed with an icy and rather cutting demeanor that I had never seen from the man before. Eventually, with a multitude of candidates sent on their way, we settled on three people who were invited back for second level interviews and shut up shop for the day. Curious about his attitude I asked what the strategy had been in dismissing some of their answers and focusing on the "what can you do for me?" format. I will never forget what he taught me that day. While education and experience are important things for a leader, what is more important is their ability to project leadership, think on their feet, and most importantly actually bring something to the dance. He looked at me with a small smile and said "Remember, I can hire graduates and even seasoned professionals all day long if I am willing to pay the right price. What I am looking for is a leader, someone who can take my place when I am not around and I will be secure in the knowledge that the company is in great hands".

Leadership by definition is the act of organizing a group of people to achieve a common goal, which means ultimately the objective of a leader is to get people to move in a specific direction with the objective of completing a set aim. There is no way of escaping this one simple fact, a leader must lead. In other words if he or she is going to be considered someone that will be able to move a team in the right direction a leader must bring something to the dance.

Influence

> *"A true leader always keeps an element of surprise up his sleeve, which others cannot grasp but which keeps his public excited and breathless."*—Charles de Gaulle

Leaders may not always be the most charming and certainly not the friendliest people in the world. What they have learned to do though is influence people and more importantly the situations around themselves in a way that creates a situation where they can lead. True leaders look for and create leadership opportunities. It is interesting to note that in certain situations a leader is willing and able to drop into a secondary role but they will not allow a loss of control over the group. Good leaders understand clearly that they are not the be all and end all of the world, and in accepting this analysis are happy to have the subject matter experts take charge as needed. That being said a leader will always be in control of the situation behind the scene when not directly leading it through persuasion, exertion of influence and a skill I have affectionately come to know as master puppeteer.

There is a fundamental difference between being in charge and being in control, a difference most good leaders are keenly aware of. Because of the innate nature of leadership mature leaders will surrender the necessity of being in charge if it ultimately allows them to be in control. For example new managers will often make sure that they lead every meeting, that their voice is heard over the rest. More mature managers understand the value in orchestrating the meeting but having people on the team lead discussions and share knowledge when they are the expert. This is as simple as having the top sales associate discuss the strategies they use to be successful or designer demonstrating the latest version of the company's products. While the sales manager could provide the training or the COO could discuss the new product having the employee that has been focused on this area exclusively lead within the meeting encourages knowledge sharing and promotes morale. Mature leaders know how to leverage the knowledge and experience within the team, orchestrating from behind the scenes. As a result many leaders are content to settle into roles where they may not be seen as the face of the company, instead taking a backseat where they can actually steer things in a more effective manner.

It is important for leaders to yield their influence carefully and in a productive manner. Leaders have the ability to influence the lives of people around them and direction of the company. This power should not be taken lightly but rather with thoughtful consideration to the impact you can have.

Intellect

> "Reason and judgment are the qualities of a leader."—Tacitus

It goes almost without saying that leadership requires the person to be in the upper spectrum of intelligence. However, for the sake of a clear understanding of what it takes to be a top notch leader, we are going to state it anyway. A leader must be smarter than the average bear. Too many times we confuse intelligence with education or IQ and while each of those are important it is equally important to remember that many leaders are simply quick learners. A key, if not the key, element to leadership is the ability to learn from ones mistakes and make adjustments in ones thinking process. Leaders are people who have gotten very good at assessing situations and making decisions based on what they know to be the smartest course of action. While they may not be the subject matter experts a strong leaders will surround him or herself with the smartest people in the field and then be the one influencing the changes.

When surrounded by a team of talented people a leader will rarely feel out of their depth. Because of the image leaders tend to project and because they have a quick learning curve, there can be a tendency for those around to overload a leader without realizing that everyone has a drop dead point. From the perspective of the leader, they will rarely turn down a challenge and as a result virtually all leaders will have gone through at least one burn out on their way to the mastering leadership. This burnout plays an important role for the leader because it teaches them the importance of knowing when to say no and when to say when.

Commitment

> *"Individual commitment to a group effort—that is what makes a team work, a company work, a society work, a civilization work."*—Vince Lombardi

No battle is won without dedication and a sense of commitment. Leaders are unquestionably committed to two things. First they are unquestioningly committed to constant growth and development both for themselves and for the teams around them. Leaders have come to understand that development is a process which can never stop and so will constantly be pushing for improvement and greater performance. They do not just expect it but personify it in leading by example. No one on the team will be pushed harder by a leader than the leader themself. As such leaders look for learning opportunities, mentorship and offer those things to the team around them.

Second leaders are committed to excellence in whatever they happen to be doing. Because second place is not good enough, because just doing enough to get by simply does not cut it the leader is dedicated almost to a point of obsession with getting it done and getting it done right. Leaders constantly look for ways to improve themselves and others because that is how excellence is achieved. As such it should not be surprising to employees when leaders demand the same of them. Good leaders also understand that employees on their team with drive and ambition will rise to the challenge of excellence they place before them.

Resulting from the highest level of commitment working for or with a good leader can at times be challenging. The leader pushes themselves and their team at an uncompromising level of ability. In this their commitment is unwavering and can seem to those less committed as being obsessive, pushy and controlling.

Vision

> *"The task of the leader is to get his people from where they are to where they have not been."*—Henry A. Kissinger

Leadership comes with a side of vision, be it ever so large or ever so small. Vision is perhaps one of the most critical elements to becoming a top of the line leader because quiet simply it is the vision which separates the leaders from the pack. Knowing which direction the team needs to go and having a clear and unambiguous idea of what forward progress looks like ultimately allows a leader to set the tone and the finish line for the team to reach and achieve. Remember that a leader's primary mandate is to lead the team toward a combined objective. It is virtually impossible without a sense of vision for a leader to take the team where they need to go.

Young up and coming leaders tend to struggle with a very delicate balance. Driven by forces within they find themselves often combatting stereo-types and a lack of vision in those around or sometimes even above them. This, unless managed correct, will result in a large degree of frustration and even some attrition as companies will often sideline a leaders thoughts because of lack of experience, age or manner of execution. Even leaders who have been around the block find that unless their vision is communicated properly confusion results and very often their ideas are simply misunderstood or not implemented because they are not the norm. One important thing to note when managing leaders is they tend to be one step ahead of the game most of the time, and it is important to channel this enthusiasm and vision in the right direction by helping them stay focused on the common goal. Because leaders are highly focused it is not hard for them to have a 10,000 foot view as well as a strong perspective on what needs to be accomplished in the trenches. Harnessing the leaders on your team, directing them and utilizing their talents will take management sharing their vision and getting them to embrace it as their own.

Image

"The leader can never close the gap between himself and the group. If he does, he is no longer what he must be. He must

walk a tightrope between the consent he must win and the control he must exert."—Vince Lombardi

One of the lessons leaders learn early on is that the image of leadership is just as important as actual leadership itself and as such have cultivated an image that projects one of profound ability. We've all been at a meeting or even just at a place of business where a person stands out from the rest. What they say or do is not necessarily all that important; rather it is the way in which they present themselves. While there is no question that leadership skills are much deeper than that which is found on the surface we learn quickly that how you are perceived often is a harbinger for the impact you will have. In order to have a profound impact a leader must project an image of strength, self-confidence and service all wrapped into one. My favorite example for this, due to its constant use in the media, is the fact that we always want our presidents to look and act presidential. What does looking presidential have to do with the man or woman's ability to run the country? Absolutely nothing, however we are drawn to those leaders who are able to create an image which demonstrates to us that they are a leader, they are the one we can follow and hence any great leaders quickly adapts to this perception and projects a leadership image.

Remember a leader is tasked with yoking a team in the pursuit of a unified goal. Unless the team is able to perceive the leader as someone who is fit to lead it will be extremely difficult to get them firing on all cylinders and the leader will spend much more time than necessary stoking the fires and keeping the passions alive. Take the example of sled dogs in the icy regions of the world. The lead sled dog is the unquestioned leader of the pack who is responsible for doing two things. First they are responsible for responding to the musher's commands (vision), find, and follow the trail. All the dogs and the sled itself follow the lead of this dog. Second the lead dog is responsible for setting the pace of the run which they do with sense of instinct and training. The other dogs will simply not follow a lead dog that seems indecisive or unwilling to lead. Lastly when a sled pulls into town no one has any question or any doubt as to who the leader of the team is.

Thinking On Your Feet

> *"Men make history and not the other way around. In periods where there is no leadership, society stands still. Progress occurs when courageous, skillful leaders seize the opportunity to change things for the better."*
> —Harry S. Truman

Leaders learn quickly that new situations arise on a daily, if not a momentary, basis. Whether a natural born leader or one that has to learn the job on the job, leaders must be able to think and react in a very short time and without much planning. While having vision is very important it is equally important for a leader to understand how to adjust fire and make ensure that there is little to no loss in momentum. Teams look to leaders when fires erupt and a leader who cannot make the adjustment finds them-selves at the short end of the stick. In essence fighting fires effectively and in a manner that hardly places a strain on the team's momentum is an essential quality for a leader to possess.

Too many leaders spend a large amount of their time fighting fires, an exercise that sucks the energy out of the leader and burns daylight. Quick thinking is not just the ability to fight a fire effectively, it is the ability to see a fire coming and take steps that will prevent or limit the scope of the fire before it ever happens. A good quarterback in football is constantly watching the field in case the planned play does not go as planned. Similarly a leader must be watching the landscape and be able to make a quick adjustment if things are not developing as they expected.

A young manager who came up the ranks of my organization was perhaps one of the best field scanners I have known. My favorite story about his team happened in the season leading up to the Christmas season. Over the past several months there has been a large increase in grumbling and general dissatisfaction among his team of retail associates at one of his stores. After taking several steps to get them back on track, including an extensive re-training initiative and a moral boosting exercise he reached the conclusion that the team was simply not willing to make the adjustments necessary and had given up on the goals. Quietly and in a manner typical of his leadership style, this young leader decided to replace three members on the team with new hires. Over the next three days he spent the time interviewing and vetting the right kind of candidates to fill these positions at a critical time when the retail world was gearing up for the holiday season. Once he had hired the right people he placed them into the store with instructions that they were not allowed to speak about their positions and were merely to learn the ropes from the veterans. Two weeks after having the teams work together; Rich walked into the store and made a startling announcement. He let the three problem children go and promoted the three new hires into full time positions. He also gave the remaining two employees a simple mandate. Either step-up and pull their weight or he had replacements for them waiting in the wings as well. Because it was clear that in having the veterans train their replacements, Rich was neither kidding nor unwilling to make the changes necessary the team flourished and had one of the best sales seasons in their history.

Leadership Styles

> *"We herd sheep, we drive cattle, we lead people. Lead me, follow me, or get out of my way."*—George S. Patton

There are a many different leadership styles and many different ways a leader guides his or her team. That being said there are four types of leaders.

- Alpha leaders are people who have mastered some of the essential skills which they need in order to successfully lead people. Because leadership is a process, Alpha leaders have learned that there is no end to the development and continue to train and improve them-selves. These leaders are also intimately aware of their own weaknesses and are very forthcoming in surrounding themselves with talent that compliments these areas.
- Beta Leaders are people who have figured out where they need to go to reach the next level of leadership but have not quite made it into the elite category of alpha leadership. Beta leaders are some of the most common in the market today. As we have faced a deluge of ways to be better leaders and a high demand for people with those natural talents beta leaders have come into their own. Always improving with their eye on the prize these leaders have an insatiable drive to be at the top of their game.
- Up and coming leaders are the next generation of leaders who are just beginning to cut their teeth in leadership. These are the mid-level and assistant managers, supervisors and team leaders who have the natural talent but still need to develop

many of the talents which will take them up the chain into beta or even alpha leadership. These leaders make excellent wing men and women because they already have the talents they need; now they just need training.

Up and coming leaders can be groomed into greater levels of position as they acquire increased skill over time. As they are they have less to offer an organization but have managed to find a way into a leadership position. The world is full of people who have been promoted far beyond their capacity and capability. While this is often the natural order of things, it is important for them to understand the type of leader they are and their current capacity. New leaders often fail to understand the damage they can cause an organization if they try to step into the alpha leader role without being ready. It cannot be said that they have no talent, much to the contrary they have an inbuilt ability to imitate good leadership. However, because this is an imitation of the real thing or a developing skill when thrown into a situation where a natural leader will shine, they may stumble along the way. Up and coming leaders that do not realize they are in the learning phase tend to be petty, self-serving and egotistical as a result of needing to maintain an image without having the skills to back it up. Many of us have had a bad taste in our mouth from being led by one of these individuals, and we all have at some point in our careers.

For the purpose of this chapter on leadership however it should suffice to be able to identify the types of leaders in an organization by doing a deep dive of their results, identifying who is really leading, taking face time with employees and finally holding their feet to the fire to demonstrate leadership.

Leadership is perhaps one of the most complicated skills to master because of its complex nature and ever changing dimensions. To young leaders I have always given this advice, learn from those who have gone before—what to do and what not to do. Study endlessly because learning never stops; a brilliant leader is constantly honing his or her skills. Finally never become locked into a box or allow outside forces to mold who you are as a leader. Life demands leaders so there is no limit to the number of opportunities out there.

Time and Time Management

> *"We must use time as a tool, not as a crutch"*
> —John F. Kennedy

Time! There just never seems to be enough of it in the day to get done all the things that need to be accomplished. Having recently retired my folks spent several years watching my son, until he started school. Several weeks into the school year my mother commented to me that she had no idea how they ever found the time in the day to watch Nathan. It was something I understood completely, because while I was working on this book and building a consulting business it seemed like the days just disappeared without much ever seeming to get done.

Most people, in all walks of life, find that time seems to get the best of them as they go about their business. Managers are certainly no exception. Much to the contrary, business owners and managers often find their time stretched to the max and will often compensate by putting in longer hours and doing things like taking work home. I am here to tell you that after years in management I never discovered the secret to getting caught up and staying caught up with all that needed to be done. Instead while driving home around 11:30 one night, realizing that yet another day was going by without seeing my children, I flipped on the radio and listened to a Toby Keith song called "My List". The idea of making time to do things that are ultimately of the utmost importance is certainly appealing but the elusive question remained how. These are a few of skill I learned that help me budget, not just manage, time.

Make a list: While this may seem a mundane and rather common place solution, this book is all about going back to basics and there is really nothing more fundamental than making a checklist. There are several important things to remember when making this list however.

1) Treat the list making like a brain storming session. In other words as you come up with things that need to be done write them down. There is no need for a particular order at this point of the planning process. The idea is to know exactly the number of things you need to get done and have them in a written form for easy reference.

2) Spend no more than 10 minutes making the list. If there is something that does not come to mind in the first ten minutes chances are it isn't super critical and you will have it on your radar tomorrow. And yes there is always a tomorrow. It is important to treat this list as a draft, the bare bones that you will add to your schedule for the day.

Over complication is an enemy you want to avoid. When making a list I used to get very detailed, using the list to actually plan the activities. This actually defeats the entire purpose of making a list. Ask any spouse who has gone shopping with a list. The list will read bread, milk and eggs not multigrain whole week bread from Safeway on isle two by the bakery which produces fresh bread around 4pm so arrive at 4:15pm in order to obtain the bread before proceeding to the egg section. Work lists should be equally compact.

Splitting you list into tasks versus things is an easy way to make the list actually seem shorter. For example if you need to document an employee's performance that would be a task, if you need to pick up staples, paper and rubber bands from Office Depot that would be under things. Why is this important? Simply put there are some things which can be grouped and done together which will save you time and make life simpler. Simplicity is ideal when it comes to making and following lists.

Lists have a shelf life of no more than one day. Once a list is made for the day the idea is to complete the tasks on the list that day, putting them off till tomorrow is a procrastination technique that has gotten many a plate overfilled. Naturally there will be things that cannot be completed today; those should go onto a to-do scratch pad (or use a calendar) not on today's list.

Finally celebrate the victories as your mark down the things completed. At heart we are all children and like children we enjoy winning games of our own making. Without compromising on work ethic or quality find a way to do the maximum number of things in a day and then attempt to do better. Doing this will give you a sense of accomplishment in your day and you will genuinely be more productive. Constantly challenging oneself is a way to grow and a great way to work through a list.

Try to avoid deviations and distractions. Life, especially in the work place, is full of distractions which is why it is often so hard to get things accomplished. List making essentially seeks to focus you on what you understand needs to get done and while you may have to deal with the occasional (or frequent fire) it is critical that once the firefighter has hung up his/her boots that you return to the list and keep going.

One final thought on lists is that mental lists are great however they do not have the potency and staying power of a written list. For some reason writing it down makes it real and lifts the sense of urgency. While mental lists are easy to carry around they are also easily lost in the various bunny trails clamoring for your attention.

Time management is about learning to budget your time in ways that get the most accomplished in the least amount of time.

While there are many wonderful books on how to manage your time better, there is one point I would like to make. While time management skills are important assets to have having the skill of time budgeting is much more impressive and ultimately more productive. They are not by any means mutually exclusive, rather are complimentary where time budgeting makes time management a whole lot easier. Time budgeting consists of two very important and equally vital parts. First is prioritizing and then setting realistic expectations of yourself and the task at hand, second is developing the discipline to stick with the budget in an almost uncompromising way.

Beginning with the list already created people learning or re-learning how to manage their time start a second important exercise, namely prioritizing and setting realistic time expectations. While there are many different methods of prioritizing, I have found the easiest and most effective method for me is using the four quadrants of importance versus urgent combined with the ABCD method.

Every task on your list falls into one of four categories. They are important, relatively unimportant, urgent, or relatively leisurely. There are two things that must be noted here. The first is that no task on your list makes it onto your list because it is unimportant, hence the distinction of important versus relatively unimportant. Relatively unimportant task are in fact tasks which need to get done, however in the current scheme of things are not a number one priority. The second distinction is the use of the word leisurely. There are many things on the list which require urgent attention; however basic human nature gravitates towards doing the things which are fun despite the fact that they may not be urgent. For myself I have always had a passion for creating dashboards, pivot tables and spreadsheets and often times found myself doodling in excel while Rome burned. Things that are in the leisurely quadrant are not necessarily "don't need to do this", they are precisely as described things that need to be done at a more leisurely pace when there is a break from doing the highly demanding items that are important and urgent.

Important: Things that are vital to day to day business fall into the important category. These are things that can range from the sublime to the ridiculous in their scope. Everything from ordering toilet paper to submitting annual reports find their way on to the important section of the grid at some point. The key distinction to remember for important items is that they are thing which are critical to doing business, making sure the company functions and ultimately the reason why you have a job. For example if you are a warehouse manager and have shipments to get out these are important and must be done before reporting or unloading new products. Why? Because customers are the lifeblood of the business so their shipments take priority. If you are a manager in the accounting department and its tax season tax preparation is important but expense reports can wait. Why? Because not filing the taxes on time could cause the company to receive fines and hurt financial performance. It directly relates to company performance and why you have a job. If you are in sales calling a prospect to close a deal is important but writing thank you cards to current clients can wait. Again it is based on what has the biggest impact on the company.

Urgent: Items in the urgent section tend to have moved their way up from the leisurely section and have been abandoned so long that they are now at critical mass and need to be dealt with immediately. Urgent items require immediate attention and must find themselves high on the priority list before they turn into a fire. Urgent items are easy to identify because they typically have a deadline associated with it and by the time it is urgent the deadline has arrived.

Relatively Unimportant: Things that need to be done but do not have a pressing timeline. For example you may want to organize your desk. That is something that needs to happen eventually but if not done within a specific timeframe nothing will be harmed. Another example could be a project that is not due until next month. You need to work on it as breaks from the "important and urgent" tasks allow.

Once you have a good understanding of the culture surrounding you, it becomes much easier to understand the way to-do's fit into the four quadrants since every manager, every company and indeed every expectation is different. If you need further direction look to the company vision, values and goals. Tasks that actively further these items are more important than those that do not.

At this stage take a piece of paper and draw the quadrant to look something like this.

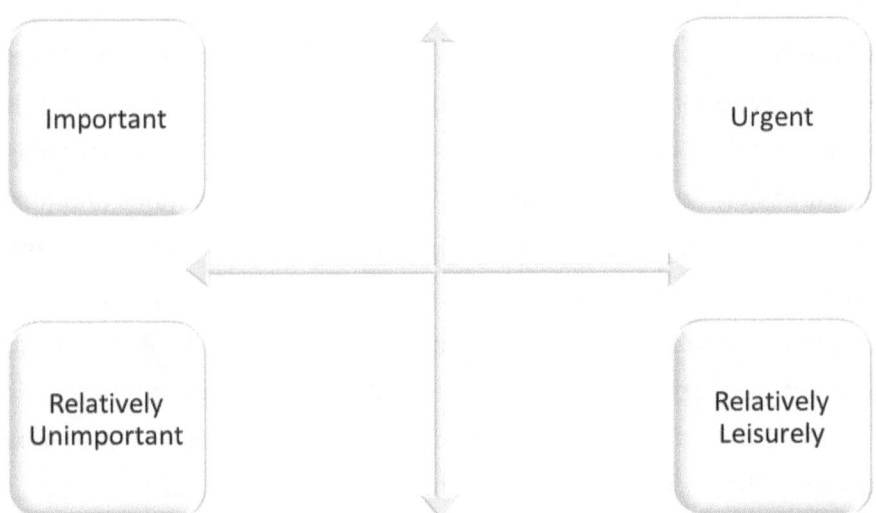

Once you have the graph in place and labeled, take the list you created and start filling in items to the various quadrants where you feel they most belong. There are only two rules to filling out the time budgeting graph.

- #1 Items can go in as many as two boxes depending on their nature and scope
- # 2 Items cannot go in contradictory boxes. For example you cannot have items that are both important and relatively unimportant because that defeats the entire purpose of planning.

With all the items listed you now have a very good idea of what need to get done and are ready to start labeling your list.

Important and Urgent are what I classify as "A" or things which must be done immediately. There should never be more than one or at the most two A's on the list. Once you are done planning your day and actually start working on it the A is the item you will address first.

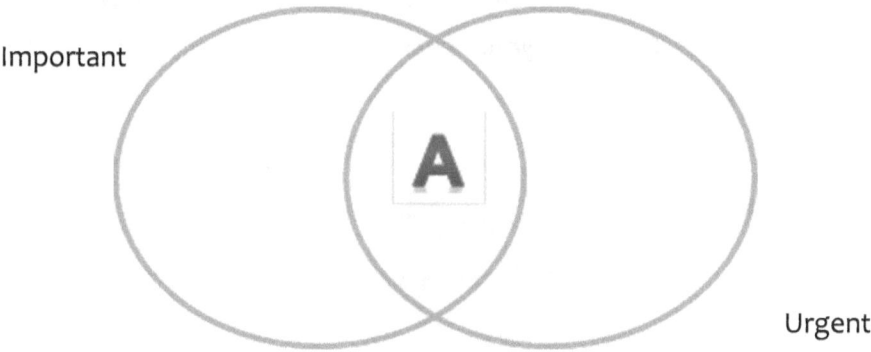

Urgent and Relatively Unimportant are classified as "B" or things that need to be done immediately subsequent to the completing of "A". Typically B's are a longer list and comprise of things that do require your attention today but are not going to sink the company if they wait for you to complete the first list.

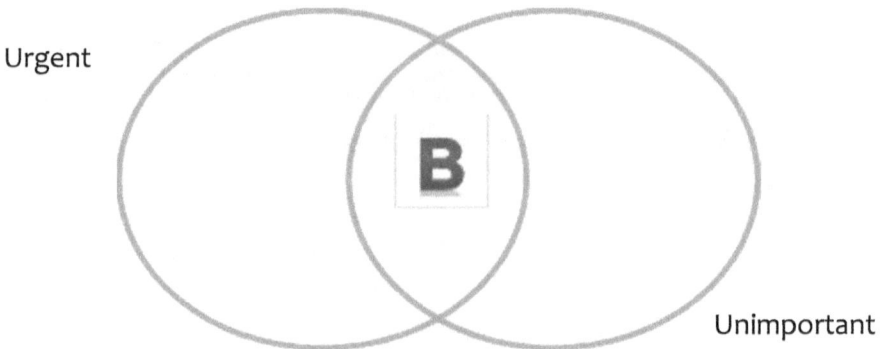

Important and Relatively Leisurely are classified under "C" as things that are important to the company's success, you enjoy doing, and typically can spend more time completing. Once the fires of A and the urgencies of B have been dealt with the items under "C" are when you pour a cup of coffee, crack your knuckles and go to work to complete.

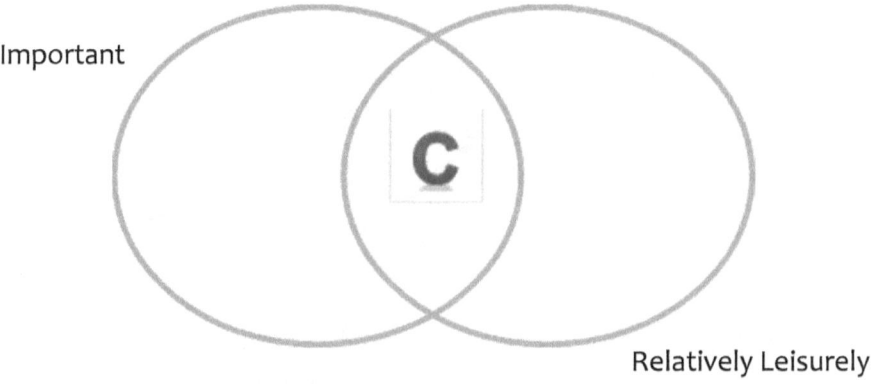

Relatively Unimportant and Relatively Leisurely are classified as "D", which in the world of management should stand for delegate diligently. These are items that really have no direct impact on the business at this stage and can be done at a slow and methodical pace. These are also excellent items to hand off to people who may not have as many A's, B's or C's on their plate and complete much more efficiently that you can. The importance of D's is to ensure that they actually get done as they have a nasty tendency to migrate north and east when ignored.

Once you have prioritized build a time schedule, I prefer to use outlook, for each item and set very clear time limits on getting things done. Remember that time limits must be realistic and you must be able to complete the task without causing yourself to have an aneurysm. Schedule you're "A" time first, then move on to "B" and so on. Once your calendar is complete give yourself 15 minute breaks in between critical items to allow yourself to refocus, recharge and get ready for the next onslaught.

It is absolutely critical that, once you have built a schedule based on prioritization and budgeting of your time that you follow it. Everything you have done thus far become irrelevant if you fail to then follow through with your own plan of action. Hence you must discipline yourself to following the plan. The upside of creating a plan and following it, other than a vast increase in productivity and loss of the deadline tension, is that your teams will start to notice how smoothly and efficiently you get things done and will start to emulate that behavior, in essence creating a culture of time budgeting and time management. Now stop for a second and imagine an entire team that processes plans and prioritizes before executing and yet the world is definitely your oyster.

One warning to managers: communicate what you are doing with your team. Employees have the habit of needing your time. This is not particularly a bad thing but can make it very difficult for managers to actually get work done. Conversations here and questions there can end up taking an entire day and before you know it 5:00 has arrived and "A" has not even been completed. One way to solve this is to establish a policy with your team that at certain hours you are unavailable for anything other than emergencies or use closing your door as a sign that you are working on something urgent and not to be disturbed.

A few years ago I worked for a large technical support company as an outside vendor for a cell phone provider. During that time their quality assurance and compliance representative gave me a book which fundamentally changed the way I looked at time management. The book was called "Eat that frog" by Brian Tracy and is a must read for anyone who finds themselves struggling to get through the daily grind. There are a few key rules that I formulated after reading this book in conjunction with the daily experiences of managing a large and rather unruly team.

> "Lost time is never found again"—Benjamin Franklin

Learn to think through your list and don't be afraid to share your tasks with your team. For many years I made lists in my head and then would quickly forget them as the rigors of the day set in. Since the lists were in my head I never got around to sharing them with the team and as a result many on the team concluded that I ran around like the proverbial chicken with my head cut off not accomplishing very much. Once you learn to share your task list with your teams you will find that they will have a much healthier dose of respect for what you actually accomplish in a day and more importantly as the team grows in strength and maturity many of your "C" and "D" things will voluntarily get pulled off your plate. Eventually even your "A" and "B" priorities will become things that are important to the team and remember teams achieve far greater results than individuals.

Pace yourself and your team based on what is realistically achievable. Striving for the moon simply because it is out there is the surest way to burn yourself out and ultimately be less productive than if you reach for the things you can do. Time is not infinite within the scope of a human's capacity for achieving work. It is therefore not a sprint in which we find ourselves, rather it is a marathon and as such only those who find a steady pace and keep to that pace can achieve success.

Finally push yourself to succeed by achieving the tasks on your list and reward yourself when you do complete them. Self-motivation is a critical element to time management because at the end of the day the list and its success or failure belongs solely to you. On days when the list seems endless it becomes important to celebrate the victories and just push on to get it done. Stopping and quitting should never be options instead when the going gets really tough, or you find yourself wishing you could quit it's time to steel yourself, say "I can do this" and plunge in.

Customer Service

"As far as customers are concerned you are the company. This is not a burden, but the core of your job. You hold in your hands the power to keep customers coming back—perhaps even to make or break the company."—Unknown

Whenever a class or a book starts with the words customer service my initial reaction is "Oh boy here we go again". Then again I am a cynic who has come to realize that most people that write training manuals and some of the books on customer service have either never worked in customer service or worked in customer service so long ago that they relate better to Noah than they do todays customer service world. So this is not going to be another monologue on how the customer is always right and how the only way to please a customer is to identify them and their needs, then bend over backwards to meet those needs. Sound different? Good.

So let's keep with the trend and make the statement that has been in the back of my mind since I started writing this book—"The customer is not always right". Say it with me and then take a deep breath and let it sink in.

The customer is NOT always right.

For years people in the customer service have heard the mantra that the customer is always right or some line that goes along with it. And as a result we have programed entire organizations to operate on the premise that an outsider, someone who tasks them with providing a service somehow knows better than the trained professionals providing that service. Now before I hear clamors that the intent of the "customer is always right" is to ensure high quality service in a non-confrontational manner, I get it. So let's look at why it is better to focus on why operating under the premise that the customer is not always right makes more sense.

According to Jamier L. Scott. (2002), "Customer service is a series of activities designed to enhance the level of customer satisfaction—that is, the feeling that a product or service has met the customer expectation."

First it is important to realize that customer service is an act which requires clear premeditation and a responsible commitment to providing the customer with service. Customer service is not a random act of catering to the customers every whim in some bizarre courting ritual that went out in the 1800's. Instead customer service requires a mindset and an attitude that is clearly focused on delivering the highest quality of service with the understanding that your job is to deliver, it is the customers responsibility to receive.

Let's delve a little deeper and examine a customer service centered mindset.

1. There are three reasons why a customer is in contact with your place of business, be it in person or on the phone or via the internet. Identifying the reason why a customer is in front of you is extremely important because each reason must elicit the correct response if the transaction is to be fruitful for both you and the customer.

    a. Most often (hopefully) customers are generally in your place of business or in contact with your place of business to acquire the goods or services which you have to offer. In other words they are there to buy something. Whether this is their first time in your place of business or they are a frequent flyer is irrelevant.

   b. The second reason a customer could be in your place of business is they have already purchased something and they want to return the product or gather a refund on the service. They are satisfied with the business but for various reasons their purchase is no longer needed.

   c. The final and most factious reason a customer could be in your place of business is they have made a purchase and are unsatisfied, which in turn has caused them to return to you in an attempt to gain satisfaction either through a refund, an exchange or simply to let you know that they are unsatisfied. As stated earlier this is by far the most factious transaction because by and large you are dealing with the customer on an emotional level where it is extremely easy to get drawn into a nonproductive interaction. We will discuss nonproductive interactions later.

2. Regardless of the type of transaction there are three primary questions that any customer service interaction must involve on your part.

   What: What has the customer come in for (remember phone conversations and internet communication are also classified as "come in's")? At the earliest stage of the conversation it is critical that you identify what exactly the customer's needs are. This will identify the type of interaction, allow you to set clear and unambiguous expectations and most importantly will allow you to provide excellent customer service.

   a. Why: Why does the customer want to . . . ? In most organizations, at all levels, we tend to avoid the question why like the plague. Why does a customer need/want a particular product or service? Many sales people don't care why as long as they purchase the product, creating a sense of get in get your stuff and get out. Understanding why a customer wants what you have to offer allows your team to provide them with the right products and services to their specific needs and an opportunity for increasing the sale. For example if you owned a plumbing company and a customer called to have a sink installed asking why could lead to the answer that they are remodeling their bathroom at which point your company could offer to help with the toilet and shower as well. By asking a basic and simple question you are able to deepen the relationship, provide the customer with what they really need and generate more revenue for the company. Customer and Company are better off by simply asking why.

Why does the customer want to return product or service? Obviously the customer purchased the product/service for a reason and then has an overriding reason why they are returning it. When I was in the cellular communications business a common reason for returns was a lack of education. Customers would purchase the latest cell phone, then confused on how to use it come back asking to do a return. Asking why would allow my team to educate them thereby offering excellent service and the customer would leave with a greater sense of loyalty because someone took time for them. The company won because time was saved, the sale was kept and a loyal customer was developed.

And finally why are you dissatisfied with the service/product which we sold you? This is a question that many a manager has tried to program into their sales / service staff and usually has to end up asking themselves. In asking this question there is always the chance the customer will let you know that the reason they are mad is your product/service stinks (in their opinion). This may be hard for your team to hear but often these opinions can be turned around by intently listening and addressing the issues. At the core disgruntled customers want to be heard and feel like what threy have to say matters. Employees and managers need to be coached to look at these situations as a challenge and not get emotional.

How can one offer excellent customer service without knowing the core reasons behind a customer's actions? In order to reach any kind of customer friendly resolution you must, repeat you must, know the why in any interaction.

   b. How: How can we as an organization or I as an individual help you to reach a resolution that is customer friendly? The question of how goes to the very core of customer service and only when this question is asked are the two parties exactly on the same sheet of music. Asking how will save a lot of time and frustration on both of your parts. The customer typically has an idea in mind and will be happy to share it with you.

3. The preset objective of any interaction with a customer, be it complaint handling or sales, is to reach a customer friendly resolution. Many people associate the word resolution with problem solving. In fact every transaction has a conclusion and therefore ever transaction has an ultimate resolution. Example: Customer walks into a retail outlet with a need to purchase a mobile phone. The sales associate does an excellent job selling a mobile phone with an additional value of two accessories.

The resolution is the customer has what he/she came in for and a solution to hands free talking as well as a protective case for the phone. It must be understood at all levels of customer service that the only acceptable resolution is one where the customer feels like they got what they came for. There is a critical distinction here that must be made, and for those of you who caught it already this will seem a little mundane. A customer friendly resolution isn't necessarily one that gives the customer exactly what they want because, remember the customer isn't always right. However a customer friendly resolution provides the customer with the feeling that they got what they came for. Ultimately the customer is there for a resolution of one kind or another and it is rare in the extreme that any customer is hell bent on a resolution of their own making. A perfect of example of this is in the banking world. A customer may come in and say they want a $10,000 credit card. After asking why you find out that they want to buy a car with it. What they need, and what you provide, is an auto loan. They did not get *exactly* what they requested but they got what they needed and therefor what they came in for.

a. A customer friendly resolution involves a large degree of input from the customer. Asking, identifying and meeting their needs is merely the first step. Actually getting the customer to work as an equal partner in the creation of the solution creates a sense of responsibility and goes very far towards having a customer believe in the solution.

b. A customer friendly resolution must be one that the customer absolutely believes in. There really isn't a plainer way to say it. If the customer leaves with even the slightest doubt that the resolution they got was not 100% what they need the resolution has failed to meet the standards of customer friendly. Aggressive? Absolutely but unless goals are set aggressively and uncompromisingly when it comes to customer service they will fail to meet the mark. Do not let the customer leave with doubts.

c. Customer friendly resolutions are uncompromising in quality. It often becomes extremely easy, especially when dealing with repeat customers, to provide an "acceptable" solution, one that isn't quite perfect but is good enough to get the job done. The customer accepts this solution because they come to believe that this is the best you can do, something that speaks very poorly of your organization in the long run. For example if a customer asks for the same product or service they always get but you now offer something better it is your duty to inform them. Yes, that would require more time and energy but providing the highest quality for their needs is essential to long term success.

d. Customer friendly resolutions are long term solutions that build value and customer loyalty. Reality check, customers do not ever want quick fix resolutions regardless of how minor their wants/needs might be. Companies and individuals that figure out that it is better to provide a long term solution from the get go build loyal customer bases of people who will never go anywhere else because they have come to expect a level of professionalism from you.

e. Customer friendly resolutions are sometimes painful and hard to swallow for the provider in the short term. Pride, ego and lack of compromise have no place at the customer service table. While the customer may not always be right,

it is important to remember that in order to provide an excellent resolution you have to be the one to do most of the giving.
4. Positive emotion and empathy are two key requirements when providing excellent customer service. The best sales people are the ones who are passionate about the product which they are selling because the enthusiasm they feel towards the product/service rubs off on the customer. Equally important is a feeling of understanding the customer's needs in a healthy and empathic manner. We can discuss empathy till we are blue in the face, most people simply don't get it. Think about it like this. When was the last time you had a problem and called in to get a resolution from a customer service center?

Let's take a classic example. Recently my in-laws, who aren't the most technologically savvy people in the word, purchased a new set of mobile phones from a large carrier. They have been customers with said carrier for about ten years now and were only talked into purchasing new phones by a sales associate who assured them they qualified for a rebate which would reduce the cost of the phones to virtually nothing. Naturally the rebate was the famous mail in kind. Since my in-laws also are not the best English speakers in the world they diligently turned over the paperwork to my wife who filled it in, dotted the I's and crossed the T's only to be told a few weeks later that the plan on which my in-laws operated did not qualify for the rebate. Apparently on the back of the receipt in the finest of prints was a stipulation that the plan must contain a data package in order to qualify for the rebate. So my wife called the service center, for some of you this sounds awfully familiar and you know exactly what is coming next. The customer service representative reiterated seven times to my wife that the stipulation was clear and since it was company policy she could not do anything to help smooth over the ill will. She did offer to add a data package for $10 per month to each phone which would then qualify the phones for the rebate. However she would not budge even when told that the sales representative who originally sold the phones would have known they didn't qualify when looking up the account (which she had to do to active new phones). What should have been a customer resolution called turned into a sales pitch and ultimately resulted in the customer screaming at the customer service person and filing a complaint with the better business bureau and the attorney general's office. Obviously not an outcome you would want for your organization. So let's look at this in terms of customer service.

    a. The customer calling in was customer number three calling because she was dissatisfied with the service. While the CSR quickly identified the problem, she then failed to adjust her delivery to meet the emotion of the moment. By being sales pitchy and condescending she made an irritated customer into an irate one.

    b. The customer service representative (CSR) knew what the client was calling in for, however she demonstrated that she really didn't care why the customer had reached a place where she needed resolution. The question of how can I solve your issue never even occurred to this particular individual.

    c. The preset objective is to resolve the customer's needs which did not happen.

    d. A customer friendly resolution would have made my wife feel like she was part of the solution (remember you cannot do this unless you are willing to ask how), it would have been something she could believe in, it would have promoted this brand as uncompromising on quality and it would have been a long term solution. For example the CSR could have been empathetic and understanding then offered a compromise where they credited the bill with half the said rebate amount. Since there was a disclaimer in place and the accounts did not qualify, my wife would have been extremely happy to receive something. The cost to the company? A little pride (admitting there could have been a problem) and a few hours of airtime. By demonstrating a positive emotion, working to reach a customer friendly resolution and by having a little empathy the CSR could have provided world class customer service.

e. Finally the customer is not always right. In this case working with my wife, who spends her day as a business analyst and understands customer misunderstandings to a tee, providing a solution that went half way and giving setting a clear understanding that the customer was not right in this instance would have actually resolved the situation. Giving in and just administering the rebate would have been the easy and wrong thing to do since it would the set the idea that all you have to do is call in and get your way.

Great customer service begins with understanding a need/desire and works its way through to a customer friendly resolution. Throughout this process perhaps the most important aspect to focus on is delivering clear and concise communication. Talking to the customer not at them, discussing things in layman's terms and avoiding industry jargon, and having a conversation not a monologue are all parts of effective communication. There are many great books written about communication in the customer service environment, and I highly recommend having a clear understanding of this level of communication. For our purposes it is important to remember to communicate and ensure understanding at all times.

Finally customer service is an ongoing and timely act. Customer service does not stop when the interaction is completed with a customer friendly resolution; instead it is just the beginning. Follow up and follow through in meeting the commitments made during the transaction are very important if the company is going to build a sustainable reputation as a customer service organization. Customer service is also timely. Most customers need or want their needs to be met quickly and efficiently. While some solutions take longer than others setting the expectation and reaching a resolution agreement with the customer must happen during the initial interaction. Once a customer understands that their need and desires are going to be met, has a clear idea of how and most importantly understands when the battle is virtually won they will become satisfied.

So let's revisit the initial assertion that the customer is not always right in the perspective of customer service as described throughout this chapter. A customer who visits a doctor because they are sick goes in with very little expectation that they are going to be the ones providing the solution, while the doctor and nurses on staff will simply agree that the customer is right and then write out a prescription. In the same vein it is unlikely that an airline is going to tell Boeing or Airbus that they need the wings on their aircraft to be made of cast iron. In both these case, which are extremely different scenarios', the customer understands that the ones providing the service or product are indeed the subject matter experts. While customers may input and have ideas they accept that their input while important may not be relevant to the ultimate resolution. However doctors will tell you exactly what is wrong with you and most will discuss a treatment plan, making you part of the solution. Aircraft companies spend month discussing aircraft with their buyers and will customize the planes as much as possible without compromising the quality and basic design. The point here is that regardless of the level or situation in which a customer resolution is needed there is always a consumer and a subject matter expert at the table. You and your company should be the subject matter expert at what you do. Therefore it is important to follow the customer service basics with a clear understanding of meeting the customer's needs, in your area of expertise. To do so does not require the customer to always be right, nor does it require you to forget everything you know in order to make the customer happy. Much to the contrary customers prefer working with subject matter experts as long as they have the opportunity to discuss the what, why and how in a positive and empathetic manner.

The most critical thing any great manager can do is build into their culture an understanding of a customer service mentality.

Motivation

"If your actions inspire others to dream more, learn more, do more and become more, you are a leader"
—John Quincy Adams

Motivation is described in the encyclopedia as the activation of goal oriented behavior. The ultimate purpose of any great manager is to get their employees to be actively involved in behaviors that are oriented towards achieving preset goals. An organization hires employees to meet set objectives whether in generating revenue, providing customer service or completing specific tasks. Since the reason why we hire and keep employees is to reach certain goals, it then becomes imperative that an organization motivate its employees and they respond to the motivation by engaging in behaviors that are goal oriented. This task falls usually to the management which quite frankly is a scary prospect.

I know throughout this book I have made statements which seem outside the box and often question conventional wisdom with the basic facts. That being said however, how can I claim that placing the burden of motivation on managers is a scary prospect?

It's actually very simple math. In most companies managers at all levels have a very clear mandate and that is to accelerate the companies production of profit in whatever area they find themselves managing. Simply put when you have a production manager, he or she is tasked with increasing the production levels, streamlining processes, maximizing potential or all of the above. Take a second and ask your management team what the three major goals for the quarter is and I would be willing to bet that a grand total of zero will tell you that one of their key goals is motivating people. While all management teams preach motivation and many companies take an active interest in motivating their people, what one finds is that when the going gets tough and the tough get going the idea of motivating the employees tends to fall by the wayside. When it comes down to crunch time, the best of managers will buckle down and drive their team to success with very little thought for motivation. And no, driving and motivating are not the same thing.

Managers that drive their employees will push them toward results in an authoritative fashion and keep pushing until the goals are achieved. Managers that motivate engage their employees to where they are active participants in achieving goals because they have a desire to be. For example driving conversations may include phrases like "or else", "you don't have a choice", "your job depends on this". Driving phrases are forceful and often leave employees feeling uneasy, unsure, and scared for job security. The goals may get achieved but employee morale and retention will suffer. Motivation on the other hand includes the employees, is inclusive, and promotes morale. Phrases and words like "together", "we", "let's achieve", "how can we accomplish this", "this will have a positive impact on your position" help an employee feel like they make a difference and motivates further achievement.

Mangers just like everyone else need to learn how to motivate and in order to do that they have to be able to know what motivation looks like, they have to know what kind of motivation to use in particular situations and most importantly they need to understand the quantitative benefits of motivating team members. Every manager in the world measures performance and in turn is measured by performance. Until companies learn to make motivation a goal it will continue to be a secondary catch phrase that is thrown around at management meetings and happens "when there is time".

So let's back it up a step and look at what precisely the subject and content of motivation is. The first and most important distinction to make from a management standpoint is that motivation is a not a noun. It is not the name of something we do when we want to increase performance or in order to maintain the current high level of performance. Much the contrary motivation is a verb, an ongoing and living action that happens every day in virtually every situation. In other words motivation is an act—an act which calls for action.

Motivation has a symbiotic relationship with both culture and with change. The higher the motivational levels in an organization the more charged the culture will be resulting in quicker and more productive changes. Lack of motivation however will cause rot to set into a culture very quickly resulting in a drop in the desire to change or improve. The reason why this is important to note is that managers and leaders often miss simple signs indicating that the culture is moving in the wrong direction, a key one is a slacking in motivation levels. For example an unmotivated employee will want to leave immediately when their shift ends. They will not be interested in learning more, improving job performance or doing more than what it takes to "just get by". A motivated employee is willing to stay an extra ten minutes to finish a task or conversation, looks for learning opportunities and works toward advancement. It is imperative for managers to notice a lack of motivation in their employees as it impacts every area of their work performance.

Motivation is a multilateral function which flows in all directions. There are no leaders and no followers when it comes to motivation, especially in a high performance culture. The perfect example of motivation being multilateral comes from geese flying south for the winter. While there is a clearly defined leader, a goose that sets the pace and the tone for the rest of the formation there is also a clear sharing of this motivationally key position. When the lead goose tires, it will be replaced by another fresher goose and will slide to the rear of the formation where it can rest and feed off the direction set by the new lead goose. Motivation works exactly the same way because providing motivation can be an exhausting job if it falls on the shoulders of a few individuals.

Motivation requires planning. Over the course of my years working in various management positions I have worked for companies that understood the importance of motivation which resulted in them spending the time and resources in training their managers in how to motivate. The thing most companies fail to do is to plan for motivation. Don't get me wrong there are organizations, especially sales organizations that do a fantastic job of motivating. The point is that while there are great courses in motivation and there are organizations and managers who motivate well it is rare for managers to actually plan their motivational exercises outside of the training room. Business is dynamic with demands placed on every employee and manager on a daily basis. Meetings get set. Customers need attention. There are fires to put out. Unless there is time planned and set aside for motivation it will often be forgotten about.

Here's a question, how many times have you walked into your work place with a specific plan to motivate a specific employee?

To motivate is to have a specific goal in mind. I have always been one of those people who has had little problem getting teams to feel motivated and even pumped up. The challenge for me has always been taking a natural sales bent and converting it into motivation that is geared towards achieving specific goals. Take for example a few years ago when while working for a massage chain, the management team set an aggressive goal of performing a certain number of massages. It took little or no effort to motivate the team into being present, performing massages or even supporting the cause. The challenge I found was translating the enthusiasm for the event into enthusiasm for results. The formula my management team came up with was this, your performance plus enthusiasm to equals to achieve these results. This is not a magic formula but it worked for me when I laid it out like so

Your Effort + Desire to achieve + Support for the Event
(Motivation) = These results

The key ingredient was making sure we set the result goal very clearly for all to see. As people got excited with the event and enthusiasm grew they understood innately that they needed to add effort that mixed with their desire to achieve would result in the results we wanted and the results were spectacular.

With my manufacturing company I found that motivation relied in inclusion. Since so many employees were not customer interfacing they did not see directly how their actions or inactions impacted the company. They knew whether they were busy or slow in their job function and if the mood in the office seemed upbeat or stressed but other than that they just came in every day, went to their desk or warehouse and performed tasks. It took a lot of effort and time to motivate them because it required translating the company's success into their success. The time spent was worth it as it drastically improved performance. For example the warehouse team needed to understand how their task of receiving orders, packing product and shipping it out quickly impacted the bottom line. Their speed and efficiency had a direct impact on cash coming into the company which helps bring in more product and ultimately pay their salary. A delay of a week from confusion or inefficiency delays payment and can cause a cash crunch.

Once they understood the impact their seemingly simple tasks had they were more motivated to be proficient. We also had some challenges with the marketing team completing tasks quickly. Since they did not work directly with customers they did not understand the impact a design or production delay had on the customer relationship. They would ask for more marketing funds to do specific campaigns and be frustrated when told no because they had not completed the customer related tasks. A lack of understanding caused conflict between marketing and sales so it had to be addressed. Speaking with both sides we sat down with the marketing team and told them how specific delays in fulfilling customer requested marketing material caused us to loose clients and what that meant in revenue. Then we were able to show them how much the campaigns they wanted to implement would cost and how the funds from those customers would have paid for the campaign and more. Seeing how their lack of performance directly hurt the company and their department caused them to understand the importance of their role in the company and it became easier to motivate them toward success. Again motivation involves including employees and instilling a sense of ownership. Taking the time to show them how they are important to the company's overall performance is vital to successful motivation.

Finally motivation must result in an increase in effort which ultimately results in an increase in productivity. In other words motivation for the sake of motivating is essentially an exercise in futility. It is important to realize that motivation and effort/results have an interdependent relationship as well. When properly executed motivation leads to an increased in effort which in turn results in more productivity. As a team sees their effort paying off in productivity and continue to be motivated the results will serve as a motivating factor for further great performance. This looks something like this.

Types and Time of Motivation

The act of motivating, if carefully planned, happens at two different times in the business cycle. These are pre-event or pre-performance and post-event or post-performance opportunities for motivating.

Every motivational event is designed around a specific performance or goal oriented behavior. By extension the act of motivating takes place in planning for the behavior to occur or immediately after an opportunity for the behavior to occur has passed with or without a manifestation of the required behavior. That sounds complicated, and I just wrote it. Let's see if we can look at it in a more simplistic way.

Pre-performance motivation is the act of motivating employees or team members before an event is due to occur. The best example of this would be the coach of a team rallying his or her players and exhorting them to give the game their best shot right before they run onto the field of play. With a sale team pre-event could include motivation before an important client presentation or meeting. With customer service staff it could be motivating them to achieve certain matrixes at the beginning of the quarter. Pre-performance motivation is easier to plan for and most people associate motivation with this aspect of it.

Post-performance motivation is the act of motivating employees or team members after the event has passed. A great example of this are the rousing speeches given by elected politicians at their victory rallies or the dumping of Gatorade over a coach whose team has just secured a major victory. Post-performance celebration as a form of motivation is also well documented and well used as coaches, managers and other leaders use the momentum of one victory to push their teams harder for the next victory. What is not quite as common is when there is a loss or a team member fails to perform the behavior required to meet the goal. Unfortunately many leaders fail to recognize that failure is a motivational moment if met correctly.

> "The greatest glory in living lies not in never falling, but in rising every time we fall."
> —Nelson Mandela

Humans by nature do not enjoy failing. That is not some deep psychological comment but a simple understanding that humanity enjoys the thrill of victory and takes no pleasure in losing. Great leaders have learned that when the human spirit is beaten if motivated correctly it will rise up more determined than ever to achieve victory. Mahatma Gandhi of India and Nelson Mandela of South Africa are classic examples of leaders who took a broken people and extolled them to victory simply by refusing to give in to self-pity, self-doubt and ultimately failure. Sports coaches are excellent at taking a beating and then rallying their teams to work hard, sweat longer and ultimately prevail because the moment of deepest loss is also a moment filled with an opportunity to motivate. The same is true in business.

Motivation comes in several varieties of which I want to look at three. While there are really no bad exercises in motivation my focus is on these three because they are very back to basic looks at motivation and are what I have used myself with effective results.

Positive Motivation: As the name suggests positive motivation is the practice of using recognition, rewards and the good old fashioned pat on the back method when seeking to motivate an employee.

This method takes performance and highlights what is good with it, celebrating victories with tangible rewards. Positive motivation can be either post performance or pre-performance. Positive motivation that is pre-performance sets goals and then emphasizes the rewards of meeting the goals. Post-performance motivation highlights the achievements after the fact and celebrates them with rewards and recognition. Often the two work very well hand in hand.

An easy way to look at pre-performance motivation is

Goal (If you meet this) = Rewards and Recognition
(I will do this)

Post-performance motivation looks like this

Achievement (You met this goal) = Rewards and Recognition
(Therefore I am doing this)

Negative Motivation: Before we discuss negative motivation it is critical to state two very important points. One because it is negative in nature does not mean that negative motivation is a bad thing which should be avoided. Second negative motivation is not a long term strategy, rather it is essential to use it only in quick win situations because long term negative motivation will soon lose its motivational factor and be left only with negativity.

Negative motivation is very often described as the stick instead of the carrot (positive motivation). Negative motivation draws very clear goals and sets consequences if those goals are not met. Negative motivation has also been used both post-performance and pre-performance; however, I have found that it is typically unproductive and counterproductive culturally to use this kind of motivation after the fact (post-performance).

Goal (Here's what we need to do)—Failure = Consequences
(Here is what will happen)

Goal setting must clearly precede negative consequence in order for motivation to be effective. Motivation is by definition a call to action. If negative motivation is to fulfill its role the subjects must clearly understand the finish line as well as the consequences for not reaching the finish line. When goals are not set there can be no call to action and hence the idea of motivation is defeated.

Fundamentally it is important to remember that people respond best to a call to action when they feel like they are part of the process. This is my favorite type of motivation since it is neither positive nor negative, and quite frankly the most effective.

Self-Motivation: Getting people to realize that they can achieve the goal because they are ultimately in control of their own destiny. Self-motivation is perhaps one of the hardest of philosophies for managers to understand and yet ironically managers are some of the best self-motivators when it comes to their own success. In order to achieve self-motivation there are three critical elements which must be addressed. First the goal must be clearly set, secondly the person who is being motivated must be part of the solution meaning that they identify with the goal and thirdly the motivator must play to the strengths of those whom he/she is seeking to motivate. Self-motivated people understand the importance of the role they play in the ultimate results of the team and company.

Different people are motivated and driven by different things. It is critical that a motivator clearly identify with what those things are in the individual they are seeking to motivate. An exercise I found to be very fruitful for me personally was to make a list of all my direct reports and next to each name list three things about them that could be used as motivating factors. Money, success, family and job satisfaction are four of the key general motivators but it is extremely important to have very specific motivational focuses with your team. If you don't have the answer as to what makes your people tick, ask what is important to them (and listen), they will be happy to tell you. For example if your employee is motivated by money ask why. It may be that they want to make their bonus because they have been planning a family vacation to Disneyland and it is the thought of their kids smiling and laughing while spending time together that motivates them. Next time you are motivating them to achieve a result you would not want to say "this will help you get your bonus". Instead you should be specific "closing this account will get you your Disneyland money". The second causes them to visualize their children's smiles while the first speaks only to a check. Which one do you think is a more motivating mental picture?

Getting people to relate to a goal is actually easier than it sounds for managers who have taken the time to know what makes their employees tick. While a manager for a linen company a good friend, who we'll call Joshua, was challenged with getting each of his hard working drivers to sell an additional $15 dollars of product weekly. For people who judged themselves on their ability to get their routes done in a certain amount of time, to maximize their earning potential, there seemed no good way to self-motivate them to take on this goal. It would certainly add unwanted minutes to their route times. Both negative and positive motivation failed to achieve the desired results. Finally he hit on the idea of self-motivation as a strategy. Instead of focusing on the rewards or consequences of the goal this innovative manager made it about the goal.

One by one he met with each of the route managers while they were out in the field and as they were making the rounds he would ask about each customer, in specific what their individual needs might be that particular day. Because most of the drivers had been running their routes for some time he got answers like "Oh Megan could really use . . ." or "John always mentions that . . ." or "I really think these guys could benefit from . . ." After several stops Josh would look at the driver intently and ask the same question "So what's stopping you from making sure that you meet the needs of these wonderful customers who you obviously have a relationship with?" The drivers had never thought that the add-on sales the company was asking for and the needs their customers obviously had were symbiotic. Once they realized that they could "sell" by simply talking with people they already liked the about solutions that they were already passionate about the rest was history.

Self-Motivation looks something like this

Involvement + Existing Strengths = Self—Motivation + Effort = Goals

Notice I sneaked effort into the equation. One cannot stress enough that any form of motivation minus effort will not yield results.

Landscapes of Failure

"Failure is simply the opportunity to begin again, this time more intelligently"
—Henry Ford

In every culture and in every organization there are things which actively work against the dreams and the direction in which success lays. From the earliest explorers who experienced moments of great frustration when sailing into headwinds or even worse having no winds at all, to politicians with great visions finding themselves stuck in bureaucracy, to the child practicing basketball all day only to find he is too short to dunk there are challenges we all face when trying to accomplish goals and advance our agenda. You and I are certainly not alone in this.

Several years ago I was working with a regional manager in a territory that could only be described as unfriendly. The managers for the client account were blatantly hostile and the area director openly supported not renewing the contract once it had expired. In the face of such opposition this regional manager remained extremely detached and almost had a surreal calm about him that often had his management team wondering if he was really connected to all that was going on around him. Launching program after failed program he never wavered in his enthusiastic support of the idea that ultimately the client would come around. Instructing his team that the client was always right, he made a habit of insisting his management team "fall on their swords" even when they were clearly on the right path. The solution he claimed was to take the higher moral ground and ensure that the client was aware of his organizations superior customer service skills. Over the course of the two years we worked together I watched him struggle within the quagmire he had created in refusing to see what was and was not reality. Had he understood that there were other solutions, including standing up for what was right the relationship could have taken a more equal turn where the client was reasonable instead of constantly demanding. Instead of chasing smoke and mirrors had the plans suggested by his managers been implemented and had he taken the time to make his people feel like they had value then the huge management turnover that he began could have been avoided. Ultimately as the division of the company wandered aimlessly from solution to solution in an endless search for that one way to get the client off the regional manager's back, he was asked to leave the company and pursue other employment. By the time this happened I had long since ceased to be a part of the organization but knowing what a great guy he was personally, it saddened me greatly to hear that he never managed to make it out of a landscape designed for failure.

No work on basics would be complete without pausing for a moment to look at, accept and work to change the very things which hold back progress. For my own personal satisfaction and with a definite sense of knowing the cliché I call them the seven deadly sins. These are places where many teams find themselves, places far from productivity and a drag on competence that ultimately leads to the best and brightest minds fleeing the ship in search of greener pastures.

The Forest

> *"A forest of these trees is a spectacle too much for one man to see."*—David Douglas

Growing up one of my favorite expressions, and my grandmother used many, referred to not being able to see the forest for the trees. As a child I always imagined a man wandering around in a dense forest, aimlessly, with an axe in hand trying to find a tree to cut for firewood. Maybe this had something to do with the fact that Robin Hood was one of my favorite stories or maybe it was a sign of things to come.

One of the cardinal sins of the professional world is the complete blindness that often seems to take control over employees and even more frequently management. Just because something seems like a good idea or a bad one does not make it so. In fact paying attention to the signs around us and the things which point to obvious success and equally to obvious failure is a critical skill in succeeding. The place where we often find ourselves among trees desperately searching for wood is when we are the ones who came up with an idea, or believe in a concept fully, and are unwilling to let it go despite all indications that something else works better.

Several years ago the owner of a multi-unit business implemented a brand new sales program which he felt would greatly increase sales in his retail stores. Being a careful man, he had consulted with corporate trainers and read many books on the subject before designing a program that was too good to fail. Implementing a diligent training program he brought each of his managers in to train them and get them onboard with the new process. Following this the organization ran several days' worth of classes to ensure that the sales associates also knew the process and had the script memorized so that they could deliver the best results. So far, so good. The problems arose later as one of the most successful of his stores, a multi-time sales award winning store, found that the manager was spending more time correcting the sales associates pitch than actually managing the performance. The level of frustration rose even higher when the owner became insistent that the sales associates learn his script verbatim and repeat it like parrots to the customer. Taking his idea further the owner, remember with the best of intentions, burned his pitch on to CD's which he handed out so that the employees could listen to them in the car, printed out flash cards to keep on each employees person and sent out a corporate inspired video to be played in the break room. Sales dipped to their lowest levels since the opening of the store and the company as a whole experienced a large percentage of employee turnover. Frustrated at the results the owner blamed the managers for failing to ensure compliance and cracking down with harsh words on the lowest performers.

What the business owner failed to realize is that his myopic viewpoint and insistence on doing things exactly his way hurt company morale, eroded culture and led to a decrease in sales performance. Some of the "signs" he should have noticed were employees quitting, feedback from management and lower sales results.

Ultimately it is key to remember that the path to success is not one which will follow a set pattern or necessarily fall in line with our ideas of the perfect road. Instead there are many forks and it becomes critical to keep a watchful eye out lest we find ourselves wandering aimlessly in the jungle of our own creation. Problems very often seem larger than life creating an aura of invincibility around them, making it critical for great leaders to quickly assess the situation and adjust course. When we start to ignore the problems simply because of an ego, fear, or because it's easier to go on blindly we truly stop seeing the forest for the trees.

The Desert Mirage

> *"Our knowledge is a receding mirage in an expanding desert of ignorance."*—Will Durant

A mirage is a hallucination off in the distance which has led many a desert wanderer to run madly in pursuit and left many a skeleton to fade into the deserts vast nothingness. Leaders often find themselves in the desert and it becomes critical to understand that mirages offer no true solutions, only a quick journey to nowhere. Mirages come in many forms from personal mirages which cause people to see themselves in a future (or a present) that is impossible to attain, and professionally where managers and employees see successes off in the distance. The key is understanding what is real and attainable and what is not. Otherwise a far greater disappointment will be had.

A local massage franchise, which I was associated with for a while, had a manager who had been in the business for over 15 years and over the course of her career had built up a reputation for being one of the wisest and most successful managers to ever cross the threshold of the business. She could do no wrong in the eyes of the owners, the corporation and herself. A wonderful success story that was unfortunately a mirage, carefully created and crafted to create an aura of success that did not really exist. It is important to note that this manager did in fact have a lot of experience and she did run one of the most rapidly growing stores in the region. However, when one dug below the surface there emerged several factors which pointed to this success being flighty and unsustainable. For one the store she ran was a brand new store in one of the most prestigious locations, meaning location had everything to do with her success. Secondly this manager had one of the highest employee turnover rates in the company, with departing employees complaining of abuse, high handedness and an overall sense of being belittled. Third the customer base universally avoided this manager and the reviews which involved her directly were atrocious. Yet she continued to be untouchable and the owners placed her on a pedestal as an example of what success looks like. When faced with the facts and numbers the owners derided those employees who had complained as being whiners, ignored the data on attrition and even expressed the opinion that the customers who didn't like this manager had to be "bad" customers who didn't fit into the culture they were trying to build. Mirages are dangerous things.

While this is an extreme story, hence why I picked it, there are all too often mirages that we chose to chase after. Images of success that are only successes in our own head and fly in the fact of data and conventional wisdom are rarely anything more than fleeting and certainly never amount to very much. Additionally they will not easily be replicated or long lasting because they are not based on skills or hard work. It is important not to confuse goals and dreams with mirages. Goals and dreams are attainable with hard work, a good solid system and perseverance. Mirages are simply illusions of success that have very little basis in reality and will suck the life out of an individual or an organization.

The Quagmire

Studying the economic model of America's recent past is an excellent example of a nation, which could be substituted just as easily with an individual or an organizations, blatant march into the worst possible of quagmires. Driven endlessly by the dream of home ownership and marching to the beat of a different rather tone deaf drummer the country allowed greed and incompetence to drive it into one of the worse financial disasters since the great depression. It should have been obvious that the road we were taking would lead only to disaster, the hindsight pundits screamed after the economy went into a tail spin. True, but it is also true that basic human nature tends to flourish in the element of risk and will often charge into a quagmire that even angles fear to tread on.

Most companies want desperately to reach the next level of success regardless of how long they have been in business. The same was true for the small manufacturing plant that had been around for roughly a hundred years. The problem was that the company while wanting to succeed was unable or unwilling to shed the practices that had caused its forward march to stall in the first place. Production had grown immensely and the new measures implemented to insure quality were having some effect. The problem was not production; the problem was a complete lack of drive when it came to sustaining a meaningful relationship with the customers. Caught up in a mentality that had taken root several decades ago, when competition was scarce, the company continued to operate under the mistaken premise that customers would put up with lack of customer service indefinitely. An excellent sales and marketing team kept new accounts flowing in the front door, and consequently kept the company in business. A lousy customer service management team, headed by a vice president who relished "telling the customer off", was pumping customers out of the back door just as fast as new ones came in the front.

Getting caught up in systems, operations and ideologies that move us nowhere is very easy to do. It is called being comfortable. The problem with comfort is that it is perhaps the most dangerous of quagmires because once you stop moving you stop growing. It has always been my belief, supported many times by examples in history, that once growth stops, stagnation and eventually rot sets in.

The Mountain

> *"Is not the mountain far more awe-inspiring and more clearly visible to one passing through the valley than to those who inhabit the mountain?"*—Kahlil Gibran

An old saying goes; if the prophet will not go to the mountain then the mountain must come to the prophet. Like the prophet mentioned here many of us believe that if we set a mountainous goal eventually we will either conquer the goal or the goal will submit and we will be victorious. While there is nothing wrong with setting aggressive and even lofty goals it is important that goals are set with a measure of humility and a healthy dose of reality.

At age 22 I decided that there was nothing I wanted more than to retire by age 30. It seemed to me like a very easy thing to do if I worked hard, made a few million and ultimately was blessed with some luck along the way. To that end I set my sites on business ownership and went about my daily life with an air of someone who had already made it. Needless to say five years into it I was starting to realize that the goal wasn't quite as simple as I had once imagined. Instead of refocusing and creating a more realistic goal I developed a giant chip on my shoulder which I carried around for several years until my wife informed me that for my age I was considered quite successful and indeed retirement at 30 was not even the privilege of the very affluent. While I sulked and pouted there slowly dawned the realization that despite having my feet often planted firmly on the ground I had allowed myself to be swept along with my own emotion and set the mountain as my goal. A mountain I might add that wasn't just out of reach it wasn't even on the same planet.

Unfortunately we do much the same thing in our professional and personal lives on an almost daily basis. Goals by definition are things which should be attainable, the must be SMART.

Specific Measurable Actionable Realistic Time-Bound

Setting goals that are specific help focus us in the right direction. Measurable goals allow us to determine how we are doing in relation to our target and let us know when we have arrived. Actionable is key because an inability to take action leads to failure regardless of enthusiasm. Goals must be time-bound otherwise it may become overwhelming in seemingly unending work. When we set goals that are specific, measurable, actionable and time-bound but fail to understand the limits of our own ability we set ourselves up for failure and disappointment. That is not to say that goals shouldn't be aggressive, much too contrary all goals should be a stretch to reach. However, they should not be so out of realm of possibility that we are left feeling like we can never accomplish them and so give up trying to succeed.

The Raging River

"Many a calm river begins as a turbulent waterfall, yet none hurtles and foams all the way to the sea."
—Mikhail Lermontov

Leaders universally tend to have one trait in common; they all have a burning desire to achieve. Regardless of the level or the place in which a leader finds him or herself they will be plagued by an insatiable desire to get better, make things better or simply drive to success. As a result many leaders have what I like to call raging river syndrome. Raging river syndrome is exactly what it sounds like a forceful body of water that sweeps on towards its destination and carries with it whatever collateral damage happens to get in its way.

One of my best friends, Jack, was a territory manager who had an up and coming attitude. He was a winner in every sense of the word who would do anything to ensure that his team stood out and won every accolade there was to offer. Jack worked harder than any person I know, often putting in twenty hour days and spending the majority of it out coaching and mentoring his team to perform better. Beloved by his team for his warmth and open love for his work, this was a manager's manager who embodied and lived success. Jack was also a raging river. In his endless quest to be the best, Jack would crush ruthlessly any signs of fatigue, weakness or non-compliance and eventually became known for his inflexibility and stubbornness. Because he had a plan and the plan had to be executed flawlessly, there was no room for argument or even disagreement if you wanted to stay a part of Jack's team. Disagreement was met with a swift tongue lashing and a reminder of who was in charge as well as what the ultimate goals were. Unable to shed the personality that dominated much of his day the same person would go home to Jack's family where his kids were expected to perform at the highest levels or face his ire.

Raging rivers rarely have control over their emotions or the consequences of endlessly driving forward. Organizations become raging rivers when driven by a leadership with that personality and will often have high burnout among its team members. Individuals with raging river syndrome rarely have good or well-balanced lives. The cautionary tale here is that while success is paramount and drive is important, tempering it with a change of pace and remembering that collateral damage is usually a sign of moving too fast makes for a much more productive and long lasting success in the end.

Bunny Trails

"I could never resist the call of the trail."—Buffalo Bill

Perhaps one of the easiest traps to fall into is that of bunny trailing and so it finds itself in dubious company as terrain you truly do not want to find yourself lost in. Bunny trailing is the practice of starting out down a concrete and established path which then quickly dissolves into wandering down side paths which may or may not have any relevance or importance to the primary route. Essentially bunny trailing can happen anytime and anywhere resulting in a waste of time and by extension serves as a distraction from the actual tasks at hand. Since this occurrence can take place at the drop of a hat and is common at every level of management it is perhaps one of the most dangerous and counterproductive of the sins.

Several years ago a well know retailer decided that they needed to polish up its image and as such set about redesigning the layout of their stores. While the idea itself was very valuable, the stores as they stood were pokey and dark places and the resulting chaos was anything but productive. The design team could not seem to come up with a single vision of what would make the stores more inviting and so came up with three different concepts. Stores across the nation were divided into the three categories based on their size, volume and age. Some stores remained in the original format; others went to a streamlined and downsized format, while still others when to the concept format or a futuristic design. Because every district had multiple stores with multiple formats the district managers and regional developers found it virtually impossible to get a synchronized effort in place where managers and store teams could help each other develop and realign their stores. The designers themselves were completely lost as to what store should look like what, and to add insult to injury the teams sending out the merchandising kits kept getting the stores mixed up. This was brain storming turned bunny trailing that ended up being implemented and going terribly wrong.

Brain storming is typically the activity that most quickly leads to bunny trailing because they are such similar activities. What becomes critical for a leader to do is remember that even in the freest flowing brainstorming session there has to be a definite goal and a method to the madness. Allowing every idea to run its course regardless of the congruity to the main theme will result in a million ideas instead of one comprehensive concept, and ultimately result in unproductive pandemonium where a cacophony of ideas are competing for center stage.

One way to ensure bunny trailing does not derail productivity is to start meetings, the day, the quarter etc with clear set objectives. Understanding what needs to be accomplished allows you to look at the options as they present themselves to determine if they will help you accomplish the goal or lead you astray.

Land of the Magic Bullet

> *"Getting rid of a delusion makes us wiser than getting hold of a truth."*—Ludwig Borne

There is no such thing as a magic bullet, let us understand that clearly and without any delusions to the contrary. Unfortunately the land of the magic bullet is one that many leaders spend their time meandering. Spending time seeking that one perfect solution, the one idea that will reshape the entire landscape is in essence a complete waste of time and resources.

As I sought a story for this section I found myself drawing a blank, simply because there are so many examples. We all have moments where we believe in that one quick fix and that is to be expected because at heart we are all dreamers. When the hope for a sudden death solution to all our problems changes into a plan, or when leaders start to actively seek that one magic bullet is when we enter the twilight zone.

This entire book is about understanding that there are key elements, basics as it were, that are the principles of success. Hard work and uncompromising commitment to finding solutions and driving endlessly towards success are the only ways to win a place at the finish, and so instead of examples I would ask that you look to your own life and find that time when you sought a magic bullet. If you found one please write me and let me know, I love success stories. If you didn't look at the solutions you did end up working on and how that panned out ultimately.

While there is no magic bullet, carefully avoiding the traps which cause failure and working on solutions that are simply back to basics ultimately will result in reward. Which road you choose to take is as always up to you.

A Final Word

"Everyone thinks of changing the world, but no one things of changing himself"—Leo Tolstoy

I started writing this book over a year ago and for the most part it was an easy recollection of things that had grown on me during a colorful career in management. A year, and many dust balls later, we finally pulled it off the shelf to re-read and publish it. In the course of that year I had started a new company and had taken on the role of the CEO and found that many of the views and ideas that once seemed so important to me had altered, if ever so slightly. Perceptions had changed and in a sense my style and approach too many of the things in the book had shifted.

Fundamentally reading the book turned out to be an eye opener for me in two senses. First I learned that many of ideas and philosophies in the book are easy to get away from when one is down in the trenches and managing people on a day to day basis. It is easy to manage by reflex instead of through a structured fundamentally planned approach. Many of the challenges that we had with the new company could, potentially, have been avoided if my own book had been part of the extensive library I refer to frequently. In essence we had forgotten to implement the very things that had worked in the past and made the same mistakes that most field generals make. In a word we were fallible.

The second lesson was far more profound, in the sense that it made me realize that no journey is ever really complete when it comes to life skills. While the philosophies of cultures and teams, leadership and time management are universal they are in fact guidelines upon which we must build our own stable platform. Back to basics provides that platform, but it is by no means the end of the journey or a magic bullet that will solve all of businesses ills and resolve all the challenges and tests that come with the responsibility of managing. My world view from being an employee and a manager is very different from my view as a CEO and the founder of a multi-million dollar company. The way the executive management team interacts with people is different, the teams are different and in essence the culture is completely different. Yet, when we went back and started to apply some of the basics principles laid out here we found that the changes from the top of the organization to the most important of employees were profound. The way we implemented them were different and unique—each management level has their own style and methods, but the results were simply astounding. As someone fascinated by the process, it was profoundly educational watching the diverse styles at work.

Back to basics is the first step in my own journey and I hope that as you have read it some of the very simple things outlined here were a reminder of how important it is to always have a strong baseline. Doing the fundamentals, leading by example, creating a culture for success—these are the exercises which never change, regardless of the size or scope of the organizations and despite personal styles, preferences and ideologies. As a result the bibliography of this book consists of influences and great authors more than just people who I have quoted.

It was a lot of fun writing this book. It was also a lot of fun going through the process of editing, removing some of the more personal and slightly antagonistic stories (which one of these days will make for a great second book), and preparing it for you, the reader. Strangely, as I mentioned, we became the very first people to actually read the book in its fullest and complete form and take something of a lesson from it. Style, personal choice and old habits die hard. I guess it is true that you can dress an old corporate male in 2012, 6th Ave fashion but take an eye off us for a second and we will go back to double pleated pants in a heartbeat.

Enjoy!

Donald Quinn

Bibliography

Baldwin, J. (1985). *The Price of the Ticket: Collected Nonfiction, 1948-1985.* New York: St. Martins Press.

Barry, D. (2004). *Wisdom for a young CEO.* Philadelphia: Running Press.

Collins, J. (2001). *Good to Great: Why Some Companies Make the Leap . . . and Others Don't.* New York: Harper Business.

Gibran, K. (1965). *The Prophet.* New York: Alfred A. Knopf.

Gladwell, M. (2002). *The Tipping Point: How Little Things Can Make a Big Difference.* New York: Back Bay Books.

Mandela, N. (1995). *Long Walk to Freedom: The Autobiography of Nelson Mandela.* Back Bay Books.

Peter, L. J. (2001). *The Peter Principle.* New York: Amereon LTD.

Turban, E. (2010). *Electronic Commerce 2010: A Managerial Perspective.* Pearson Education.

www.ingramcontent.com/pod-product-compliance
Lightning Source LLC
Chambersburg PA
CBHW030759180526
45163CB00003B/1093